The Great Big Book
of
Fun Phonics Activities

by Claire Daniel, Deborah Eaton, and Carole Osterink

SCHOLASTIC
PROFESSIONAL BOOKS

New York • Toronto • London • Auckland • Sydney • Mexico City • New Delhi • Hong Kong

Dear Teacher,

Nothing can be more important in the primary grades than instilling in children the joy of reading and teaching them the skills to become successful, lifelong readers. To do this, we must teach children how to unlock the mysteries of print. Reading instruction that includes systematic and explicit phonics instruction is essential to achieve this goal.

Phonics instruction unlocks the door to understanding sounds and the letters or spelling patterns that represent them. Quality phonics instruction engages children, provides opportunities for them to think about how words work, and offers reading and writing experiences for children to apply their developing skills. The playful, purposeful activities in *The Great Big Book of Fun Phonics Activities* offer practice, reinforcement, and assessment of phonics skills. In combination with your daily reading instruction, these activities will help to capture the fun and excitement associated with learning to read.

Enjoy!

Wiley Blevins, Reading Specialist

Cover Design: Vincent Ceci, Liza Charlesworth, and Jaime Lucero
Cover Illustration: Abby Carter
Interior Illustrations: Renée Andriani, pp. 269–296; Rick Brown, pp. 213–240; Abby Carter, pp. 5–16, 101–128; Shelly Dieterichs, pp. 44–72; Rusty Fletcher, pp. 129–156, 297–352; Cynthia Jabar, pp. 241–268; Becky Kelly, pp. 185–212; Judith Pfeiffer, pp. 157–184; Carry Pillo, pp. 17–44; Jill Weber, pp. 73–100

Series Development by Brown Publishing Network, Inc.
Editorial: Elinor Chamas
Interior Design and Production: Diana Maloney and Kathy Meisl

Contents

Auditory & Visual Discrimination

Using This Book

Classroom Management

Reproducibles Reproducible pages 9–16 offer a variety of individual and partner activities. Answers to the activities are provided below, as necessary.

Directions You may wish to go over the directions with children and verify that they can identify all picture cues before they begin independent work.

Games When children play partner games, you may want to circulate in order to make sure children understand procedures.

Working with the Poem

A poem on page 8 introduces the phonics element in this book, auditory and visual discrimination. Start by reading this page aloud to children. You may want to duplicate the poem so children can work with it in a variety of ways:

Echo Reading As you recite the poem, line by line, act it out. Have children echo the words and imitate the action.

Rhyming Words Recite the poem and have children supply each fourth line, the one that ends with a rhyming word. Have children identify the words that rhyme (*floor, more; knee, see*).

Visual Discrimination Write the poem on a chart. Ask volunteers to circle the beginning consonants, words, or even whole phrases that match.

Innovation Have children extend the poem by adding new verses. To begin, brainstorm names of body parts and possible rhyming words—for example, *head, instead; chin, again; feet, seat; toes, goes.*

Teacher Notes

Page 8 *Answers:* Cat face—Children add three whiskers, one eye, and one spot; House—Children add one window, a chimney, and one bush.

Page 9 *Answers:* Bottom picture—chef hat, oven mitt, muffin tin.

Page 11 *Answers:* Add star T-shirt, giraffe T-shirt; add striped socks, plain socks.

Page 12 *Answers:* Sunny-day Bear—sunglasses, sandals, hat, ice-cream cone; Rainy day Bear—umbrella, raincoat, rainboots.

Page 13 *Answers:* 1. b; 2. d; 3. p.

Classroom Fun ...•••

Auditory & Visual Discrimination

What's New?

Use this game to develop visual discrimination and oral language. Begin with a simple outline drawing of an animal, leaving out details like eyes, ears, nose, markings, and so on. Show the picture to the group and be sure everyone gets a good look at it. Then without anyone seeing, add a detail to the picture and show it to the group again. Have children tell you what was added. Take another turn yourself. Then give children a chance to add details and challenge their classmates to tell what they added.

What's Alike?

Have children take turns locating two things in the classroom that are alike in some way. The two things might be the same color, about the same size, have names that begin with the same sound, or share some other characteristic. The child points out the two things and asks: "What's alike about _____ and _____?" The rest of the class must guess the answer.

Make a Pattern, Break a Pattern

Use construction paper squares of two different colors or sizes to create various patterns. Lay out each pattern, repeating it three or four times, and invite children to study the arrangement of squares and figure out the pattern. Then ask children to close their eyes while you remove one or more squares. Ask children to open their eyes and have a volunteer put back the missing pieces.

Quick Change Artists

Make use of the dress-up box in the Dramatic Play Center for this activity. If you have a screen or some other kind of partition, use it to create a dressing area. Have children go with a partner to dress up with items from the dress-up box, and then show their costumes to the whole group. When everyone has observed what they are wearing, the two should go back to the dressing area, and each of them should remove or add one costume item. When they return to the whole group again, children must guess what's different about their outfits.

Listening to Sounds

Assemble a number of different things that make sounds. Use obvious sound makers, like bells and rhythm band instruments, as well as less obvious noisemakers like cellophane and pencil sharpeners. Ask children to close their eyes and listen as you make two sounds in a row. Invite children to tell you if the two sounds were the same or different. As a variation, have children guess what item you used to make each sound.

Sound Patterns

Ask children to listen as you make a series of three sounds that the children can replicate. Have children repeat the sounds in the same order. Repeat the process several times with different series of sounds. Then invite the children to take turns making patterns of sounds for the rest of the class to echo.

Variation: Make a series of three sounds. Then repeat the series, leaving out the last sound. Ask children to make the sound you omitted.

Name _____

Hands Up

Reach for the ceiling,
Touch the floor.
Stand up again,
Let's do more.
Touch your head,
Then your knee,
Up to your shoulder,
Like this, see.
Reach for the ceiling,
Touch the floor.
That's all now—
There is no more.

Directions: Children will enjoy exercising both mind and body as they listen to this poem and follow the directions. Try turning it into a chant! See page 6, "Working with the Poem," for more ideas.

Name _____

The Big Race

Look at the pictures. Tell the story to a friend.

Directions: Go through the story with children, asking "What happens next?" and tracing with your finger the order of the pictures as you go. Pair children up and encourage them to tell one another the story, tracing the order of pictures with a pencil. Finally, have them color in the page.

Name _____

What's Missing?

Directions: Tell children to look at the top half of the page, at the two cat faces. Ask children to figure out what is different about the picture on the right. What is missing? Tell children to draw the missing features to make both pictures the same. Then have them do the same with the house pictures at the bottom of the page.

The Great Big Book of Fun Phonics Activities © Scholastic Professional Books

Name _____

What's Different?

Directions: Tell children to look a the top and bottom pictures. Are they exactly the same? Tell children to color the three things they see in the bottom picture that are not in the top picture. Then encourage volunteers to describe what is happening in the scene.

Name _____

Decorate a Headband

Draw the shapes that finish the patterns. Then color your headband.

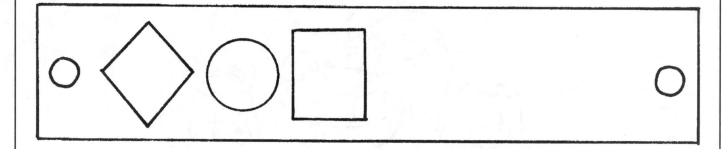

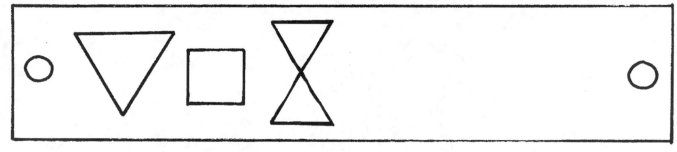

Directions: Have children work with a partner. Encourage them to discuss the patterns and then to help each other draw shapes on the headbands to complete each pattern. Then have each child choose one of the headbands to color, tie strings to, and take home.

The Great Big Book of Fun Phonics Activities © Scholastic Professional Books

Name _____

Hung Out to Dry

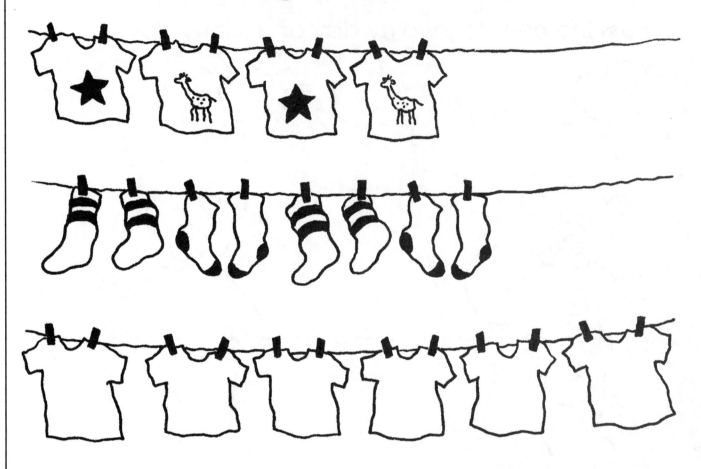

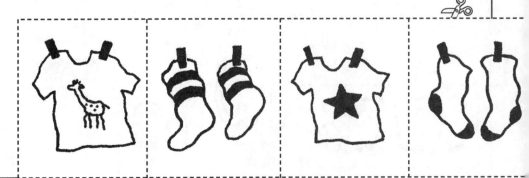

Directions: Ask children to describe the pattern they see on each clothesline. Tell them to cut out the pictures at the bottom and paste them in place to continue each pattern. Then have them color or design the T-shirts on the last clothesline in a pattern of their own choosing. Finally, have them exchange papers with a classmate and describe the classmate's pattern.

Name _____

What Should the Bear Wear?

Dress the bear for a rainy day or a sunny day.

Directions: Have children cut out and paste the appropriate clothing items on the rainy day bear and the sunny day bear. Then invite children to color the pictures.

The Great Big Book of Fun Phonics Activities © Scholastic Professional Books

Name _____

Match the Sound

1.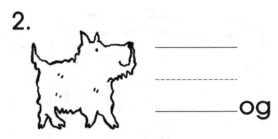

_____
- - - - - - - - -
_____ear

2.

_____
- - - - - - - - -
_____og

3.

_____
- - - - - - - - -
_____ig

4. My name

_____
- - - - - - - - - - - - - - - - - -
_____

Directions: For items 1–3, have children look at each picture, say the animal's name, and then write the letter that begins the animal's name on the line. Then have children draw or paste a picture of something else that begins with the same letter in the space under the animal's name. For item 4, have children write their own first name and then draw or paste something that begins with the same letter as their name.

Name _____

Picture This

Directions: Have children name the things they see in each framed picture. Make sure children understand that the two items in each picture have names that rhyme. Then have children draw a picture on the blank canvas that illustrates any two words that rhyme. Invite volunteers to tell about their rhyming pictures.

The Great Big Book of Fun Phonics Activities © Scholastic Professional Books

Alphabet

Using This Book

Classroom Management

Reproducibles Reproducible pages 21–33 offer a variety of individual and partner activities.

Directions You may wish to go over the directions with children and verify that they can identify all picture cues before they begin independent work.

Games When children play partner games, you may want to circulate in order to monitor their responses and their understanding of procedures.

Working with the Poem

A poem on page 20 introduces the phonics element of this book, the letters of the alphabet. Directions on that page will get you started with ideas for presenting and enjoying the poem. Here are a few more ideas for extending the experience:

Personal Response
Reread the poem and have children respond to the question at the end. Use this discussion as an opportunity to talk about the relationship of words to sounds and sounds to letters.

Matching Letters
Write the poem on the chalkboard or on chart paper. Using plastic letters or the Letter Cards on pages 42 and 43, have children match the letters in the poem to spell CAT, DOG, and COW.

Innovation
The names of many letters rhyme with *T* and *G*, so it will be easy to expand the middle part of the poem to include more examples of things that can be referred to by spellings instead of sounds.

Connecting School and Home

The Family Letter on page 19 can be sent home to encourage families to reinforce what children are learning. Children will also enjoy sharing the Take-Home Book on pages 35–36. You can cut and fold these booklets ahead of time, or invite children to participate in the process. You may also want to mount the pages on heavier stock so that you can place the Take-Home Book in your classroom library.

Letter Card Set

Pages 42–43 of this book contain matching sets of uppercase and lowercase Letter Cards. You may wish to mount these on heavier stock as a classroom resource. You may also wish to duplicate and distribute them to children for use in matching and sorting activities. Each child can use a large envelope to store the cards.

Assessment

Page 34, Show What You Know, provides children with targeted practice in standardized test-taking skills, using the content presented in this book in the assessment items.

Dear Family,

Your child is learning in school about the letters of the alphabet. Being aware of the connection between sounds and letters is the basis for success in learning to read. You may enjoy sharing some or all of the following activities with your child:

Letter of the Day

Work through the alphabet, one letter a day, and make a game of identifying that day's letter on signs and labels throughout the day.

Sound to Letter

Make talking about letters and sounds part of your everyday conversations. For example, if you're out together and your child points out a dog, make the point that *dog* begins with *d*. Then together think of some other words that begin with *d* like *dog*.

Reading Together

As you read your child's Take-Home Book, "Picking Letters," together, encourage your child to name letters of the alphabet and to say the sound each letter stands for.

You may also wish to look for these books in your local library:

Chicka Chicka Boom Boom
by Bill Martin, Jr. and John Archambault

Albert's Alphabet
Leslie Tryon

Sincerely,

Talking Letters

What if, when you opened your mouth,
Instead of sounds, letters came out?

If you called a pet that purred C-A-T,
And you called a pet that barked D-O-G,

If you said milk came from a C-O-W,
Well, you'd be talking letters, wouldn't you?

Directions: Read the poem aloud. Invite children to practice what their names would be if they "talked letters." See page 18, "Working with the Poem," for more ideas.

Name _____

A is for ant.

A a

A

a

B is for bee.

B b

B

b

A   a   B   b

Directions: Help children identify the *ant* and the *bee* and trace the letters *Aa* and *Bb*. Have children cut out the letter boxes from the bottom of the page. Have them paste *A* and *a* on the signs the ants are holding. Have them paste *B* and *b* on the signs the bees are carrying. Encourage children to suggest names for each ant (Andy, Alicia) and each bee (Bob, Bonnie).

Name _____

C is for cat.

D is for dog.

Directions: Help children identify the *cat* and *dog* and trace the letters *Cc* and *Dd*. Tell children to look at the letters on the children's T-shirts and on the animals' tags. Tell them to decide which letters match, and then to draw a leash line to connect each child to the right pet. Then children may color the picture.

Name _____

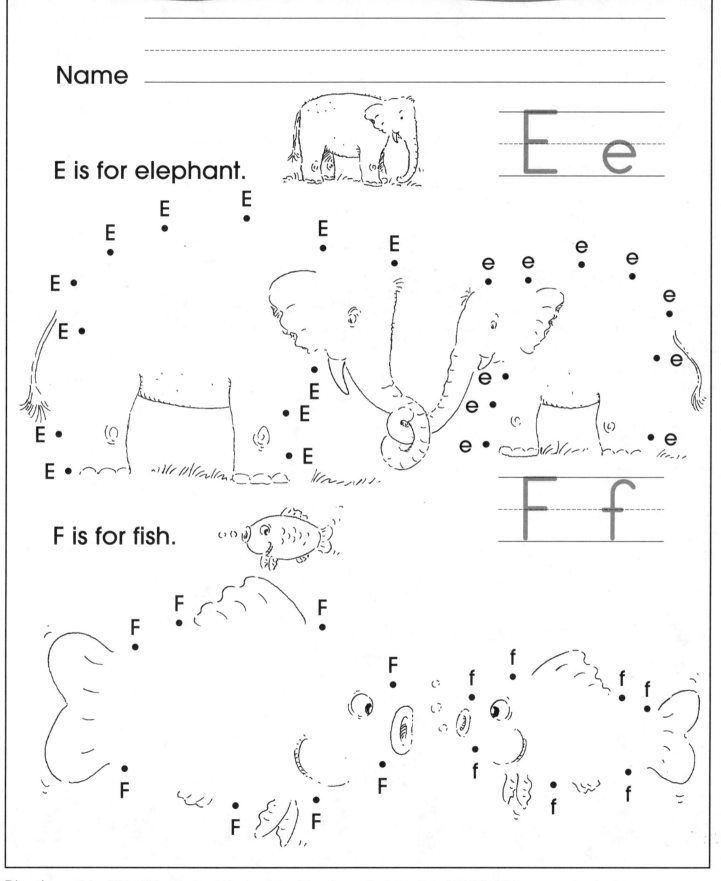

E is for elephant.

E e

F f

F is for fish.

Directions: Help children identify the *elephant* and the *fish* and trace the letters *Ee* and *Ff*. Tell children to connect the dots next to the capital *E's*, and then to connect the dots next to the lowercase *e's*. Ask what they see. Then have them connect the capital *F's* and the lowercase *f's*. What do they see this time?

Name _____

G is for goose.

G g

H is for hen.

H h

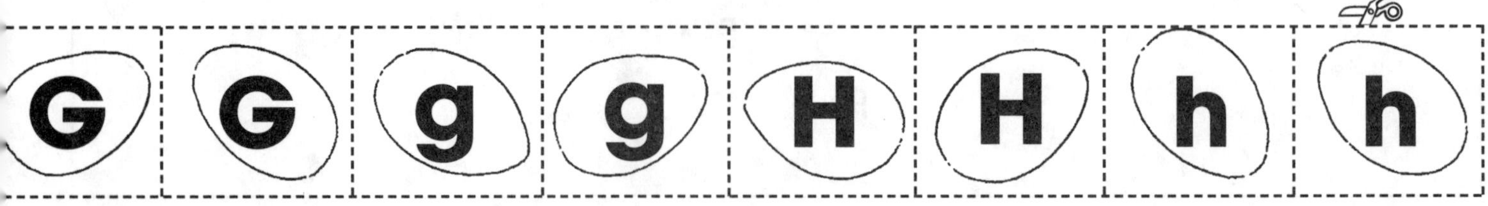

| G | G | g | g | H | H | h | h |

Directions: Say the names of the animals, *goose* and *hen*, with the children. Have them trace the letters *Gg* and *Hh*. Then have them cut out the boxes containing the eggs. Tell them to paste the eggs with *G* or *g* in the goose's nest. Tell them to paste the eggs with *H* or *h* in the hen's nest.

Name _____

I i

I is for inchworm.

I f

I I

I h

I j

I i

I i

J j

J is for jellyfish.

J j

I j

J J

J f

J i

J j

Directions: Identify the *inchworm* and the *jellyfish* for children, and have them trace the letters *Ii* and *Jj*. Then have children look at the two letters on each inchworm's leaf. Tell them to color the inchworms that have the letters capital *I* and lowercase *i*. Then have them look at the letters on the jellyfish, and color the jellyfish that have the letters capital *J* and lowercase *j*.

Name _____

K is for kangaroo.

K k

L is for llama.

L l

K k   K k

L l   L l

K k

L l

K k

K k

K k

K k

L l

L l

Directions: Identify the names of the animals, *kangaroo* and *llama*, with the children, and have them trace the letters *Kk* and *Ll*. Tell children to trace the *Kk* path to help the baby kangaroo find its mother. Then have them trace the *Ll* path to help the baby llama find its mother.

Name _____

M is for monkey.

M m

N is for newspaper.

N n

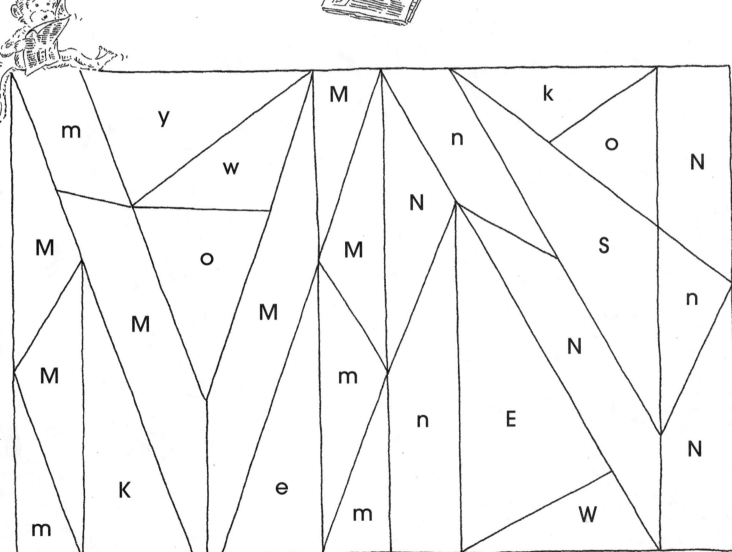

Directions: Help children identify the pictures of the *monkey* and *newspaper*, and have them trace the letters *Mm* and *Nn*. Then tell children to look at all the letters inside the box. Have them color all the shapes with *M* or *m* in red and all the shapes with *N* or *n* in blue. Ask children what they see.

Name _____

O is for otter.

O o

P is for penguin.

P p

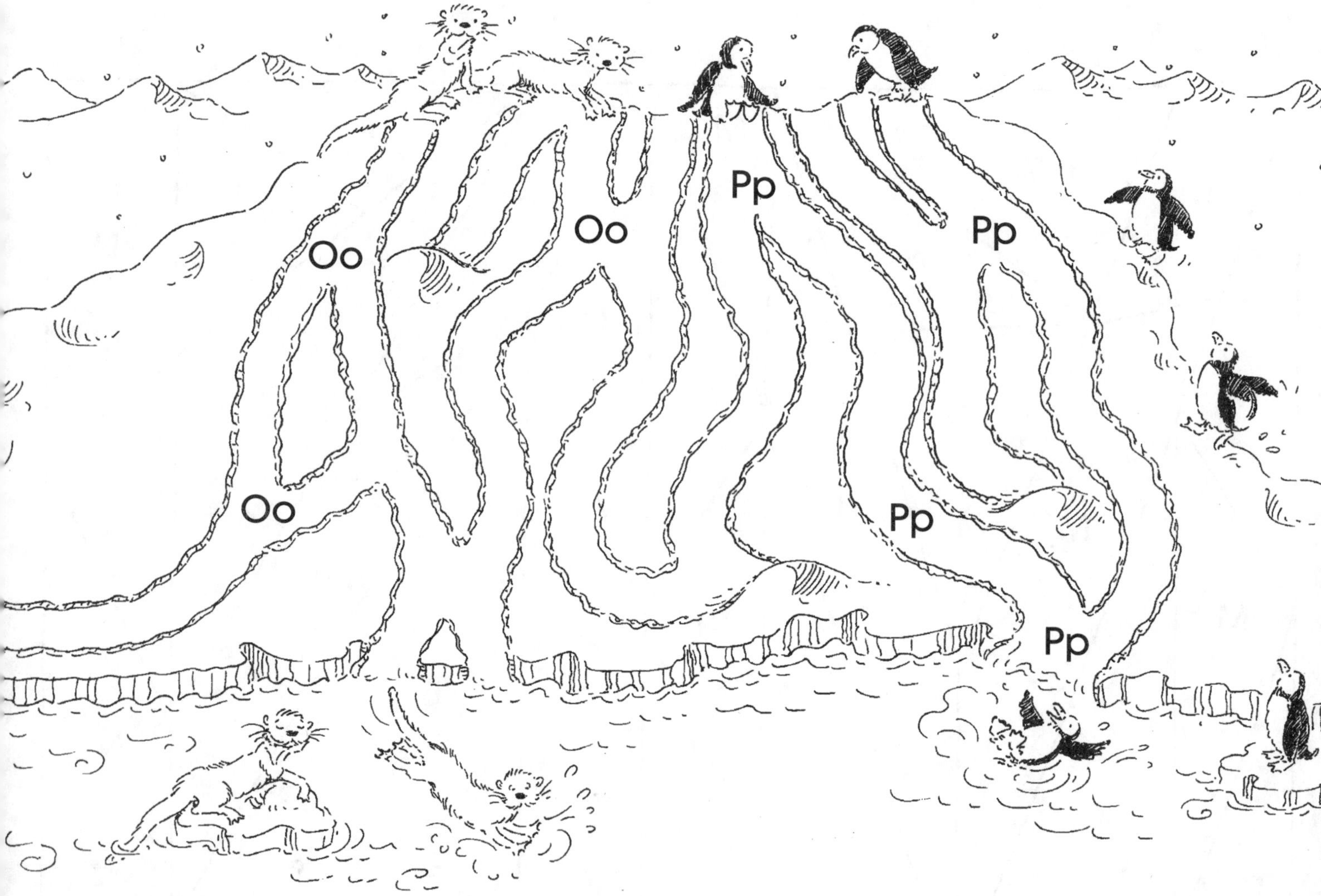

Oo   Oo   Pp   Pp

Oo   Pp   Pp

Directions: Help children identify the *otter* and the *penguin* and trace the letters *Oo* and *Pp*. Have children draw lines along the *O* and *o* paths to help the otters find their otter friends. Then have them draw lines along the *P* and *p* paths to help the penguins find their penguin friends.

Name _____

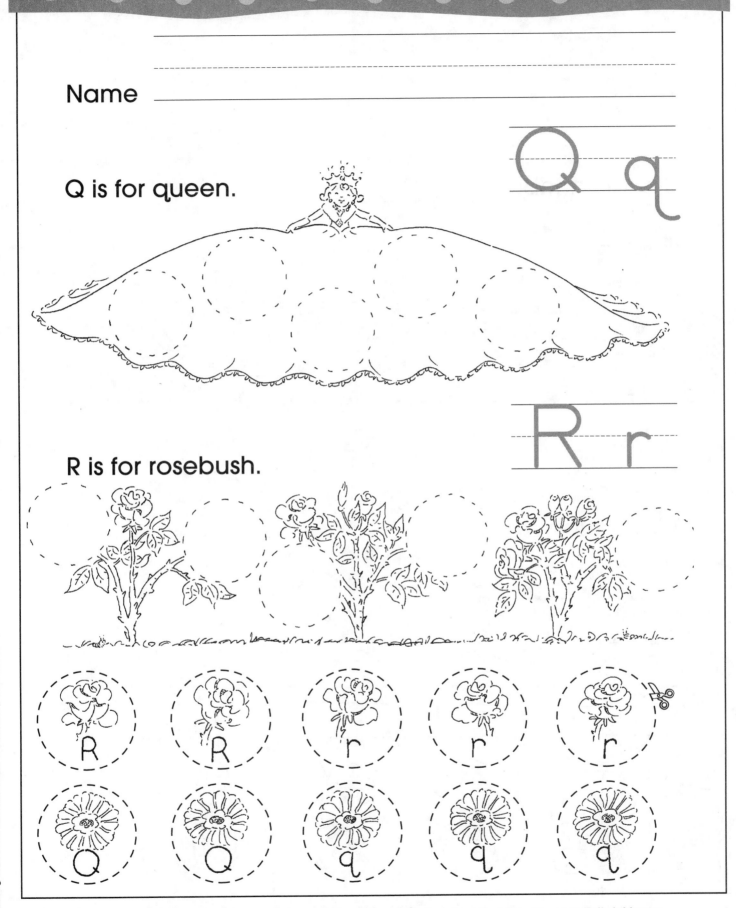

Q is for queen.

R is for rosebush.

Directions: Help children identify the *queen* and the *rosebush* and then have them trace the letters *Qq* and *Rr*. Tell children to cut out the flowers. Have them paste the flowers with *Q* or *q* on the queen's skirt and paste the flowers with *R* or *r* on the rosebush.

Name _____

S is for sandbox.  **S** s

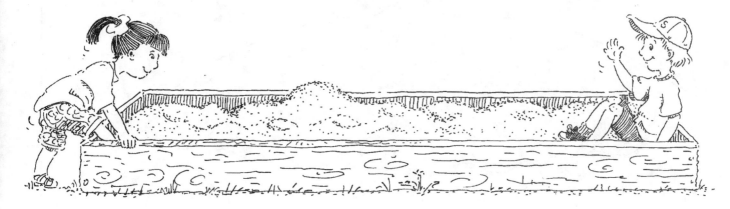

T is for tub. 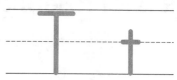 **T** t

Directions: Help the children identify the *sandbox* and the *tub,* and then trace the letters *Ss* and *Tt.* Tell the children to cut out the boxes with toys. Tell them to paste sand toys with *Ss* tags in the sandbox and tub toys with *Tt* tags in the tub.

Name

U is for umbrella.

U u

V is for vegetables.

V v

U   u

V   V

U   u   V   V

Directions: Help children identify the *umbrella* and the *vegetables,* and have them trace the letters *Uu* and *Vv*. Tell children to cut out the small pictures. Have them match up the letters on the small pictures with the letters in the scene and paste the pictures where they belong.

Uu, Vv   31

The Great Big Book of Fun Phonics Activities © Scholastic Professional Books

Name _____

W is for walrus.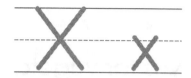

X is for exit.

Directions: Help children identify the *walrus* and the *exit* and have them trace the letters *Ww* and *Xx*. Tell children to find and color the two animals wearing the letter *W*. Have them put an *X* on the two doors marked *EXIT*.

Name _____

Y is for yak.

Z is for zebra.

Y y

Z z

Directions: Help children identify the *yak* and the *zebra*, and have them trace the letters *Yy* and *Zz*. Tell children to look for and trace the hidden letters *Yy* and *Zz* on the ice rink. Then have them draw other ice skaters and color in the scene.

Name _____

Show What You Know

1. A   ○ C   ○ A   ○ B   ○ H

2. D   ○ D   ○ L   ○ P   ○ U

3. K   ○ F   ○ C   ○ H   ○ K

4. M   ○ N   ○ G   ○ M   ○ A

5. T   ○ E   ○ T   ○ O   ○ I

6. s   ○ i   ○ s   ○ r   ○ c

7. e   ○ u   ○ t   ○ e   ○ s

8. b   ○ t   ○ b   ○ c   ○ p

9. n   ○ h   ○ m   ○ o   ○ n

10. z   ○ z   ○ h   ○ s   ○ a

Directions Tell children they will practice taking tests. Tell them to read the letter of the alphabet next to the number in each row. Tell them to find a letter that is just the same in that row and to fill in the circle in front of that letter.

The Great Big Book of Fun Phonics Activities © Scholastic Professional Books

Oh no! There they go!

8

1

I have Q, R, S, and T.

6

I have E, F, G, and H.

3

I have A, B, C, and D.

2

I have U, V, W, and X, Y, Z.

7

I have I, J, K, and L.

4

I have M, N, O, and P.

5

Classroom Fun .....

Alphabet

Letter Collections

Write each letter of the alphabet at the top of a separate sheet of chart paper. Display all the sheets around the room at a level where children can reach them. Then invite children to collect letters. Whenever they find a big letter in a magazine or a newspaper, they should ask for permission to cut it out and bring it to school. Encourage children to collect letters every day. Set aside time in class each day for children to paste letters on the appropriate sheet.

Alphabet Walk

Take a walk around the school and the surrounding neighborhood looking for letters. Begin by looking for an *A*. When someone spots an *A*, make certain that everyone sees it before you move on to look for a *B*. Continue looking for letters in alphabetical order, retracing your steps if necessary, until all the letters have been located, from *A* through *Z*.

Body Letters

Invite children to work with a partner to come up with ways to form letters with their fingers, their hands, their arms, or their whole bodies. Have children demonstrate their letter formations for the rest of the class to see if the others can guess what letter they are making.

Fifty-Two Pick Up

Create letter cards from a deck of playing cards by covering the faces with letters. Make a card for every uppercase letter and one for each lowercase letter. Children can use the cards to play a matching game. The object of the game is to find pairs of letters—uppercase and lowercase. Each player starts with five cards. On each turn, each player draws one card. Play continues until all the letters have been matched.

What Can It Be?

Ask children to select a letter and write it on a piece of paper. Then have them transform the letter into a picture of something. A *C*, for example, could become the tail of a cat; an *M* could become a mouse. Invite children to show their finished pictures to the rest of the group and have children guess what letter each classmate started with.

Classroom Fun

Match a Letter

Have pairs of children play a letter-matching game using the Letter Match Game on page 41. Players will also need a number cube, two markers, and a set of plastic capital letters. To begin, children place their markers on START. They take turns rolling the number cube and moving their marker the number of spaces shown. They must find the plastic letter that matches the letter they land on, or a letter that is written somewhere on the walls of the classroom.

Create a Dictionary

Have children create their own dictionaries. Help children staple or bind thirteen pieces of paper together to form a booklet. Have them label each page with the upper- and lowercase forms of a different alphabet letter. On each page, they can write words they know that begin with that letter.

Letter Quilt

Have children create a letter quilt. Give each child a large square of colored construction paper. Have each child write the capital and lowercase forms of a letter on the square and decorate it with pictures of items whose names begin with the letter. Tape the finished squares together, adding plain colored squares as necessary, to form a quilt. Display the quilt on the classroom wall.

Class Alphabet Book

First, assemble a collection of alphabet books for children to enjoy at their leisure. Here are some unusual examples of the genre you may want to look for:

ABC Drive! A Car Trip Alphabet by Naomi Howland
Robert Crowther's Incredible Animal Alphabet by Robert Crowther
Action Alphabet by Shelley Rotner
Alphabet City by Stephen T. Johnson

When children have had a chance to examine several examples of the genre, invite them to work together to create a class alphabet book. Encourage children to choose a theme for their book. Assign the letters and help children select key words for their letters. Then have children create individual pages to contribute to the class alphabet book.

Letter Count

Conduct a survey to find out which letter appears most often and least often in children's names. Go through the alphabet, from *A* through *Z*, and have children raise their hands if that letter appears in their first names. Use tally marks to record the count. Review the results together. This could be a good opportunity to introduce the distinction between vowels and consonants.

Making Letters

Have children form tactile letters. Children can:

- Bend pipe cleaners to form letters. The letters can be glued on pieces of tagboard and displayed so children can trace the letters with their fingers.
- Write letters using white glue or paste. Have children sprinkle glitter or sand on the glue. When the glue dries, children can finger-trace the letters.
- Write a letter on a piece of paper. Have children trace over the letter with a glue stick and place things like cotton balls, confetti, or yarn along the path of the glue.
- Form letters in trays of damp sand.
- Dip a small piece of sponge into finger-paint and make sponge prints along the outline of a large letter.
- Use their fingers to form letters with finger-paint.

Picture Cards

Invite children to help you create a set of alphabet picture cards by cutting pictures out of magazines or drawing illustrations to represent each letter. Mount the pictures on oaktag and store them in envelopes or folders. You may want to use words suggested in the Word Bank on page 44. Here are a few ideas for using the picture cards:

- Hold up a picture card. Have children find the letter card (from pages 42–43) that stands for the beginning sound of the picture name.
- Display a letter card or write a letter on the chalkboard. Have the children identify picture cards whose names begin with that letter.
- Hold up a picture card. Have children find an object or a word written in the classroom that begins with the same letter as the name of that picture.

Instant Activities

Line Up by Letter Use letter order to line children up in a variety of ways. One day, have children line up in alphabetical order by first name, another day by last name or in reverse alphabetical order.

I Spy Whenever children leave the classroom as a group, to go to the playground, the gymnasium, or the library, assign children alphabet letters to look for along the way.

Secret Letters To help children recognize letters, finger-trace letters on children's palms and have them tell you what letter you formed.

Alike and Different When you are writing on the chalkboard, use the opportunity to help children explore the similarities and differences between pairs of letters: For example, **F, E; C, G; O, Q; P, R; P, B; V, W; a, g; g, q; b, d; i, j; h, b; r, n; n, m; v, y.**

Eating the Alphabet Plan snacks to include foods that begin with the letters of the alphabet in alphabetical order—apples, bananas, carrots, dates, eggs, and so on. Involve children in planning what the next snack should be.

Upper and Lower Write words on the chalkboard in all capital letters. Invite children to rewrite the words using all lowercase letters.

I Am Thinking Play a guessing game with children. Select some object in the room and give clues about it. Make your first clue one that tells the beginning letters in the object's name: "I am thinking about something whose name begins with *B*." Offer more clues and let children ask questions until they are able to guess what you are thinking of.

Alphabet Chant Have children take turns leading the class in a creative alphabet chant, similar to a cheer at a sporting event. For instance, Child Leader: Give me an *A!*—Class: *A!*, or Child Leader: *A, B, C, D*—Class: *A, B, C, D* and so on.

Letter Match Game

z	Start	b	c	d	e
End a					f
y					g
x					h
w					i
v					j
u					k
t					l
s					
r	q	p	o	n	m

Letter Cards

a	b	c	d
e	f	g	h
i	j	k	l
m	n	o	p
q	r	s	t
u	v	w	x
y	z		

Letter Cards

A	B	C	D
E	F	G	H
I	J	K	L
M	N	O	P
Q	R	S	T
U	V	W	X
Y	Z		

Word Bank

Below is a list of words that you may use to illustrate the letters of the alphabet. All the letters are included in the Letter Card Set on pages 42–43. Ideas for using these cards and additional cards you may create yourself can be found in "Classroom Fun," pages 37–39.

Alphabet Letters

A a	E e	I i	M m	Q q	U u	Y y
alligator	egg	iguana	milk	queen	umbrella	yak
ant	elephant	ink	mittens	question	uncle	yard
antelope	elevator	inchworm	moon	quilt	under	yarn
apple	enter	insect	mouse	quiet	up	yo-yo

B b	F f	J j	N n	R r	V v	Z z
ball	fan	jacket	nest	rabbit	vest	zebra
banana	fence	jar	newspaper	rainbow	vine	zipper
bear	fish	jelly	nurse	rock	violin	zigzag
beetle	fox	jump	nuts	rooster	van	zoom

C c	G g	K k	O o	S s	W w	
cat	garden	kangaroo	octopus	sand	walrus	
carrot	girl	kitchen	ostrich	sandwich	wagon	
caterpillar	goat	kite	otter	seal	window	
cow	goose	kitten	ox	sun	woodpecker	

D d	H h	L l	P p	T t	X x	
dance	hamster	lemon	pet	tiger	box	
desk	hand	letter	penguin	toad	fix	
dinosaur	hat	lion	pig	tub	fox	
dog	horse	ladder	pizza	turtle	six	

Beginning Consonants

Using This Book

Classroom Management

Reproducibles Reproducible pages 49–61 offer a variety of individual and partner activities.

Directions You may wish to go over the directions with children and verify that they can identify all picture cues before they begin independent work.

Games When children play partner games, you may want to circulate in order to monitor that responses are correct and procedures have been understood.

Working with the Poem

A poem on page 48 introduces the phonics element in this book, beginning consonants. Start by reading this poem aloud to children. Duplicate the poem so children can work with it in a variety of ways:

Echo Reading Recite the poem, line by line, acting out the poem as you go. Have children echo the words and imitate the action.

Visual Discrimination Write the poem on a chart. Ask volunteers to circle each consonant letter and a word that begins with the same beginning consonant, such as *D, Duck.*

Dramatization Assign one line per child, and have children perform a dramatic reading of the poem. You may prefer to have children learn their assigned lines by heart. Encourage the child playing letter *B* to make a very dramatic appearance!

Connecting School and Home

The Family Letter on page 47 can be sent home to encourage families to reinforce what children are learning. Children will also enjoy sharing the Take-Home Book on pages 63–64. You can cut and fold these booklets ahead of time, or invite children to participate in the process. You may also mount the pages on heavier stock and place the Take-Home Book in your classroom library.

Word Card Sets

Pages 70–71 of this book contain matching sets of Word and Picture Cards drawn from the vocabulary presented in this book. You may wish to mount these on heavier stock as a classroom resource. You may also wish to duplicate and distribute them to children for use in matching and sorting activities. Each child can use a large envelope to store the cards.

Assessment

Page 62, Show What You Know, provides children with targeted practice in standardized test-taking skills, using the content presented in this book in the assessment items.

Dear Family,

Your child is learning in school about beginning consonants.

boat   **k**ey

Learning letters and sounds is an essential step in learning to read. You may enjoy sharing some or all of the following activities with your child.

Home Labels

Use sticky notes to label familiar items in your home with the beginning consonant of their names. Encourage your child to read these labels and to write or dictate labels for other home objects.

Letter Hunt

Choose a letter of the day and help your child look around the house for objects whose names begin with that letter. Invite other members of the family to join in the hunt. Post a list of items you have all found.

Reading Together

To practice recognizing beginning consonants, go over your child's Take-Home Book, "The News at the Zoo." Ask your child to point out or circle the beginning consonant in the name of each animal in the story and say it out loud.

You may also wish to look for the following books at your local library:

Happy, Hiding Hippos

Babette McCarthy

The Piggy in the Middle

Charlotte Pomerantz

Sincerely,

Name _____

Letters on the Run

I'm Afraid! called A.
Duck Down! said D.
Go on! Go on! cried letter G.
N and O just shouted NO!
P Paused, but Q was Quick to go.
Yipes! said Y, Zipping close to Z . . .
Unless I'm wrong, here comes a B!
BUZZZZZ!

Directions: Read the poem to the class once or twice. The next time you read, have children raise their hands or stand up each time they hear the name of an alphabet letter in the poem. See page 46, "Working with the Poem," for more ideas.

Name

Roll-a-Letter

Here's a rainy day word game to make and play.

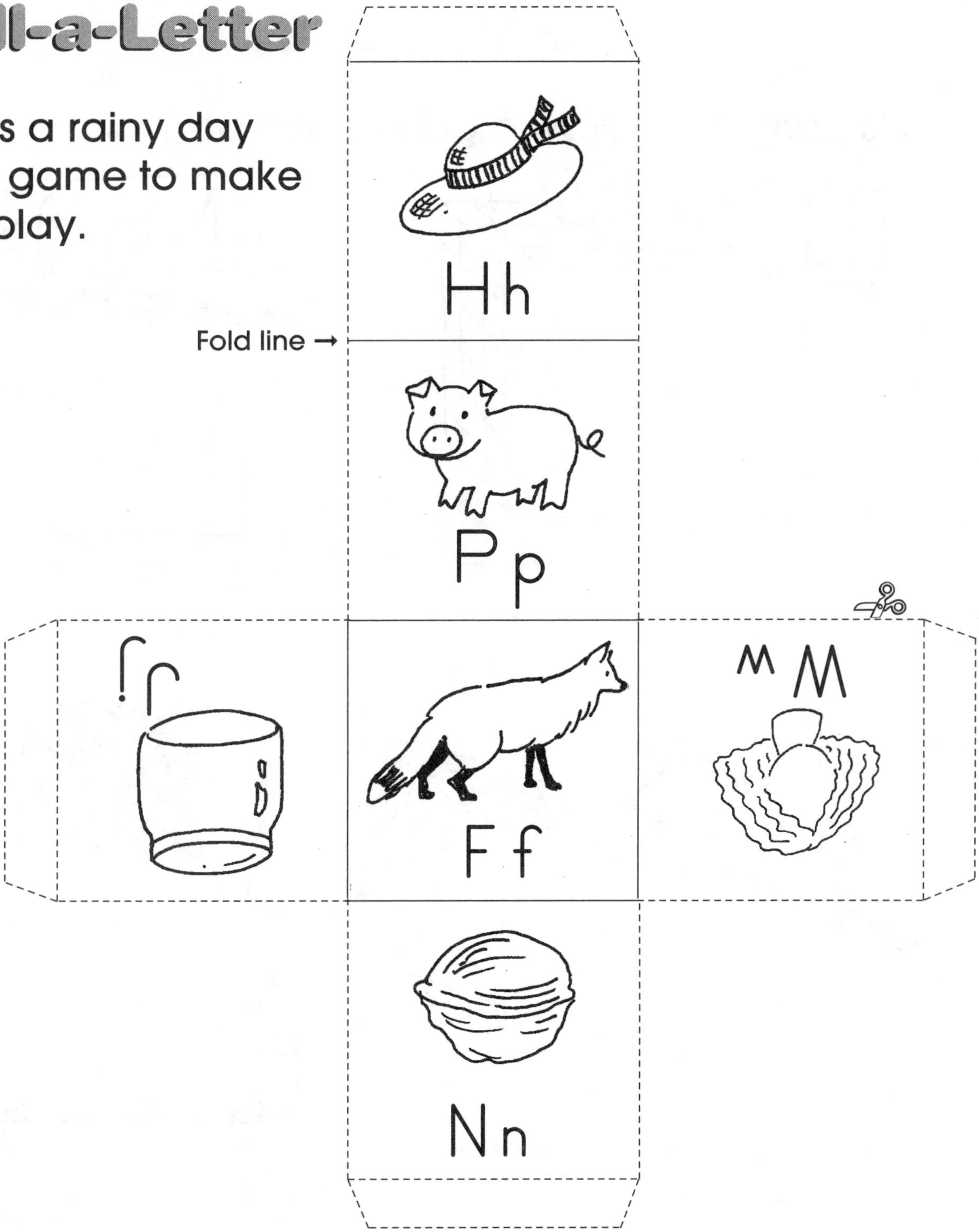

Fold line →

Hh

Pp

J j

F f

M M

N n

Directions: Have children play this game in pairs or small groups. First, make up the letter cube. Glue the page to lightweight cardboard and cut out the cube. Fold it and tape it together. Have children take turns rolling the cube. Tell them to name the letter that shows on top, as well as another word that begins with the same sound/letter. A child receives one point for each new word named. The first player to have five points wins the game.

Name _____

Gift Boxes

It's party time! Draw a gift in each box.

Directions: Review the letters and their sounds. Instruct children to draw a gift in each box whose name begins with the sound on the tag. Children dictate or write the name of each gift on the line.

Name _____

Bear-Bear

It's cold outside. Cut out the clothes. Dress Bear-Bear.

Directions: Have children cut out the squares and paste them on the bear, matching beginning sounds and letters. Then have them color Bear-Bear and his clothes.

What's That Sound?

| Bb | Pp | Rr | Ww | Yy | Zz |

Directions: Go over the picture names with children. Tell them to say each name aloud, choose the letter from the letter box that stands for the beginning sound of the name, and write it on the line in the speech bubble. Finally, have children color the page.

The Great Big Book of Fun Phonics Activities © Scholastic Professional Books

Name _____

Fill It Up!

Fill up the containers.

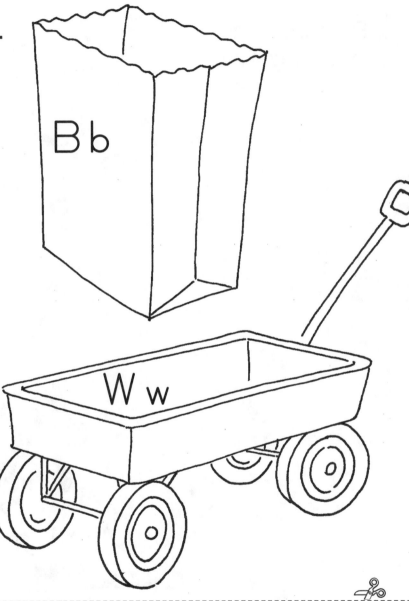

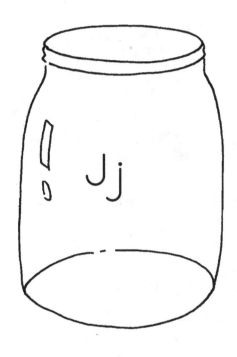

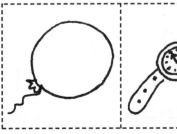    

Directions: Instruct the children to cut out the squares, say the names of the items to themselves, and match them with the container whose name begins with the same sound. Have them paste the squares in the correct containers.

Name _____

Letter Match

Find out who is acting silly.

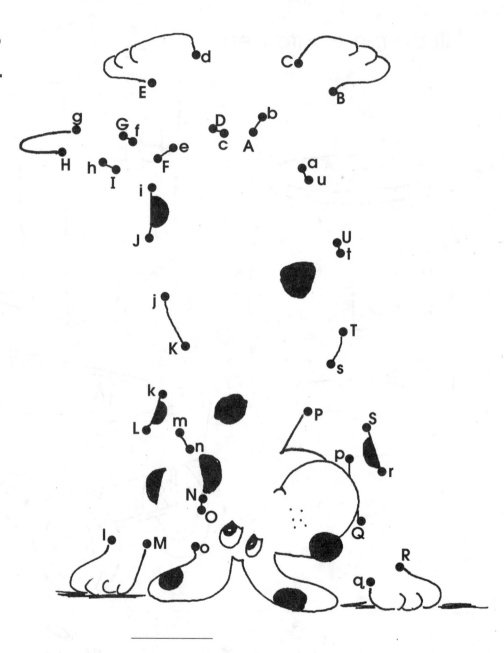

The _____ og is on his _____ ead.

Directions: Ask children to look for letter matches and to draw lines between the matching capital and lowercase letters. When they have completed the picture, they can complete the sentence by adding beginning consonants. Then encourage children to color in the picture.

The Great Big Book of Fun Phonics Activities © Scholastic Professional Books

Name _____

Whose Toy Is It?

It's time to play!

_____ adio

_____ ebra

_____ oll

Dan

Rosa

Zeb

_____ uck

_____ oo

_____ obot

Directions: Read the names on the children's T-shirts aloud. Explain that each child only plays with toys whose names begin with the same sound as his or her name. Have children write the appropriate consonant to complete the name of each toy. Then have children draw lines from each child to the matching toys.

Name

Picture This

What belongs in each box?

Bb

Rr

Ff

Dd

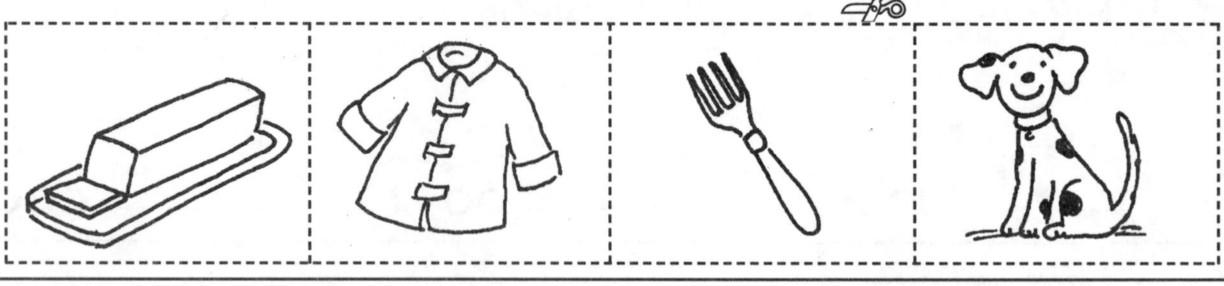

Directions: Ask the children to look over the page, read the letters in each box, and brainstorm what might belong in each picture. Then have children cut out the small pictures, say the name of each picture, and paste each one where it belongs.

The Great Big Book of Fun Phonics Activities © Scholastic Professional Books

Name _____

Make Your Own Story

Tt

Cc

Directions: This activity can be completed individually or in pairs. Talk about the pictures with the children. Have them cut out the story pieces for each letter, move them around, talk about them, and make up a story. Encourage children to paste their pictures on a piece of paper in story sequence. Be sure they understand that they don't have to use all the pieces. Ask volunteers to tell their stories to the class.

The Great Big Book of Fun Phonics Activities © Scholastic Professional Books

The Alphabet Zoo Game

This zoo is empty. Can you fill it up?

Bb	Cc	Dd	Ff	Gg
Ww				Hh
Xx				Jj
Vv	Yy	Start Here / Start Here	Zz	Kk
Tt				Ll
Ss				Free Turn
Rr	Qq	Pp	Nn	Mm

The Great Big Book of Fun Phonics Activities © Scholastic Professional Books

bat	camel	deer
fish	gorilla	hippo
jellyfish	kangaroo	lion
monkey	newt	panda
quail	rabbit	swan
tiger	vulture	walrus
ox	yak	zebra

Directions: This game may be played by two or three players. You will need a number cube and one small distinguishable marker for each player. Go over the animal names with children. Have children cut out the animal cards, and place their markers in the center of the gameboard. Players deal out all the animal squares. They take turns rolling the number cube and moving their markers in any direction. If a player lands on a letter for which he or she has a matching animal card, the card is placed on the letter. The first player to place all of his or her animal cards wins the game. Individual children may also play the game, pasting the animal squares on the board until the board is complete.

Make Your Own Bookmarks

Make these bookmarks. Then use one as you read a book.

Directions: Have children cut out the boxes and paste them on the bookmark that matches the beginning consonant sound. Encourage children to use the bookmarks in school and to take one home to use with library books.

Name _____

Hidden Letters

B, C, D, F, G, H, J, K, L, M, N, P, Q, R, S, T, V, W, X, Y, Z

Directions: Look over the pictures with children. Tell them to say the name of each picture aloud, and then look within the picture for the hidden letters that stand for the beginning sound of that name. Have children circle the hidden letters and then write the letters on the lines. Encourage children to create their own hidden letters picture in the empty box.

Name _____

Show What You Know

Say the name of each picture. Fill in the circle next to the letter that stands for the missing sound. Write the letter on the line.

1. ○ d ○ b ○ y ____ uck	2. ○ q ○ x ○ p ____ ueen	3. ○ v ○ w ○ t ____ est
4. ○ b ○ p ○ h ____ at	5. ○ g ○ c ○ j ____ at	6. ○ p ○ f ○ d ____ ish
7. ○ l ○ k ○ h ____ ite	8. ○ x ○ z ○ y ____ ebra	9. ○ r ○ n ○ m ____ ope
10. ○ t ○ l ○ h ____ ape	11. ○ g ○ r ○ s ____ oat	12. ○ r ○ b ○ j ____ ike

Directions: Go over the instructions with children, showing them how to fill in the circle.

The Great Big Book of Fun Phonics Activities © Scholastic Professional Books

Shh. Don't wake up baby!

8

The News at the Zoo

1

Wake up, tiger.

6

Wake up, kangaroo.

3

Wake up, monkey.

2

Wake up, panda.

4

Roar

7

Wake up, camel.

5

Classroom Fun .....

Get Aboard the Consonant Train!

Make a big train with one car for each consonant. Each car can be a piece of brightly-colored construction paper, with paper plate wheels and a letter written near the front of the car. Staple the sides and bottom of each car to a bigger piece of paper. Place the cars around the classroom at a height children can reach. As you study each consonant, children can draw pictures or cut out pictures from magazines to fill each car. Discuss the car contents with children occasionally to review each letter.

Consonant Quilt!

Assign each child a consonant, and distribute sheets of construction paper and other art materials. Ask children to write their assigned letter and decorate the sheet with pictures whose names begin with the sound of that letter. Cut out long strips of a contrasting color, to place between the pages. When you tape or staple all the letters together, you will have a consonant quilt to display in the hall or classroom.

B Is for Beanbag

Divide a large sheet of drawing paper into sections, and write a consonant letter in each section. Then challenge children to a beanbag toss. Have them take turns tossing the beanbag onto the paper. The child must say the name of the letter in the section the beanbag has landed in, along with a word that begins with that letter. Players earn one point for each new word.

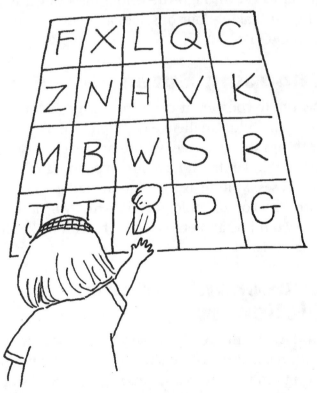

Tongue Twisters

With the class, brainstorm words that begin with a particular consonant letter. Write each word on a big index card. Let children take turns closing their eyes and rearranging the cards. Then read the words aloud in the random new tongue twisting order and have children attempt to say the words after you.

Classroom Fun

Play "OOPS!"

This game uses the consonant cards on page 69. Choose the letters you would like the children to review, at least 8 at a time. Have children play the game with partners. A child turns over the squares one at a time. As each letter is revealed, the child must name it and say a word that begins with that letter. If the child is successful, he or she can move to the next letter. If not, the other player writes a big O on a piece of paper. The object of the game is for one player to get through the whole stack of cards without making four mistakes and ending up with O-O-P-S!

Shopping Spree

Distribute consonant cards from page 69, one for each child. Challenge children to make a list of things they will buy whose names begin with that letter. Let them have fun expanding their purchases, as long as they use the letter correctly. For example, for the letter *Nn*, "new car" would be acceptable. See who can make the longest list.

Consonant Picture Dictionary

Work with children to make a consonant picture dictionary. Start with a simple photo album or a 3-ring binder with plastic insert pages. Set aside a page or two for each consonant. Place a cut-out consonant letter inside each section. Encourage children to make drawings or find pictures they can cut out of magazines whose names begin with that consonant. Have them continue to add pictures to the appropriate section in the consonant picture dictionary throughout the school year.

Consonant Charades

Divide the class into competing teams. Prepare index cards with letters and action words. You can get some ideas from the Word Bank on page 72. Here are some to try:

   Ww—wash windows
   Rr—row a boat
   Vv—vacuum the room
   Pp—paint a wall
   Hh—hang out clothes

Distribute one card at a time to each team, and quietly help the team read the action words as necessary. Have the team act out the word, as the other team tries to guess what it is.

Letter Stories

Encourage children to tell and write "letter stories" independently, with partners, or in small groups. To help children practice letters and sounds, you may want to brainstorm words that begin with the target letter. Here are just a few story-starting ideas:

   Letter L is Lost!
   H has the Hiccups!
   How can We Wake Up W?
   D has Disappeared!
   R Can't Stop Running
   S Is So Silly!

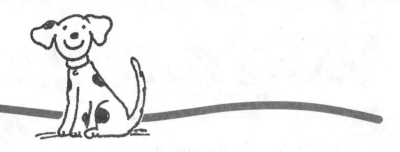

Fish for Letters

Cut out fish shapes from colored paper or gift wrap. Write a consonant on each one. Clip a big paper clip to each fish. Place all the fish shapes in a box or paper plate. Then use a ruler and string to make a fishing pole. Tie a small magnet to the end of the string. Have children take turns fishing for letters. If a child can say the letter and think of a word that begins with the sound that letter stands for, he or she can keep the fish. The player with the most fish at the end of the game wins.

Consonant Baseball

Place four chairs around the room to serve as first base, second base, third base, and home plate. Organize the class into two teams. When the first team is "up," the first player sits at home plate. You are the pitcher: Write a consonant on the board. The player must then name the consonant and a word that begins with that letter/sound. If the player answers correctly, he or she moves to first base. If not, the side is out, and the other team is up. Teams make points when a player advances all the way around the bases. A player may take more than one base at a time by giving a two or even three-word answer, such as "B—baby boy."

Letters Checkers

Paste consonant letters on the black squares of a checkerboard. You can cover every square, or just a few. Two versions of each letter, one facing in each direction, will allow both players to see the letter equally well. Children play checkers as usual, but with one difference. Before moving to a square, they must be able to name the letter and its sound. To make the game a little more difficult, instruct players to name the letter, its sound, and two words that begin with that letter/sound.

Put This on File

Challenge the children to help you fill a file box with consonants. Bring in a cardboard file box with alphabet dividers, and remove the vowels. As you study letters in class, invite the children to find words and pictures whose names begin with that letter sound. You may want to post a copy of the Word Bank from page 72 for children's reference. Have children draw or cut and paste pictures on the file cards. When it's time for review, you can just pull out the cards for that letter.

Instant Activities

I Spy Say, "I see something that begins with the letter *B*." Children guess until someone names the item. Then that child takes a turn at thinking of an "I Spy" object.

Consonant Charades Act out a word for each consonant. Tell the class the beginning letter and challenge them to guess the word. (Examples are bounce for *B*, cough for *C*, dig for *D*, and so on.)

Shiny Consonants Pass out index cards. Assign each child a consonant letter. Have each child write the letter in glue and shake glitter on it. Display the shiny consonants on the chalk tray.

Letter Tag Distribute the consonant cards from page 69. Divide the class into two teams and have them line up on one side of the room. The first child on each team must place his or her letter next to something in the room that begins with that letter, then run back and tag the next child in line. The team that is first to place all of its letters correctly wins the game.

Play "A My Name Is Alice." Children can take turns, going all the way through the alphabet.

"A my name is Alice. We live in Alaska. And we sell apples."

"B my name is Bonnie. We live in Boston. And we sell butter."

Ghost Letters Have each child trace a consonant letter on a partner's back. A correct guess means the partner gets a turn to trace a letter.

Consonant Party Begin the game by saying, "Let's have a consonant party. I'll bring bananas to the party." The next person must offer to bring something that begins with another consonant, such as "raisins." If you want to make the game more challenging, ask players to answer cumulatively: "I'll bring bananas and raisins to the party."

"The Wheels on the Bus" Sing the popular song "The Wheels on the Bus." Ask children to help you come up with new verses that have repeating consonants, for example:

"The tubas on TV go toot, toot, toot..."

"The bees on the bus go buzz, buzz, buzz..."

"The worms in the wood go wiggle, wiggle, wiggle..."

Consonant Cards

B	C	D	F	G
H	J	K	L	M
N	P	Q	R	S
T	V	W	X	Y
Z				

Directions: Cut out the letters. You may want to back them on cardboard or laminate them. Use them for a variety of games, including the games described in "Classroom Fun" and "Instant Activities."

Word Cards

ball	cow	duck	fish
gum	hat	king	milk
nest	pig	queen	rope
sock	tie	wagon	zebra

Picture Cards

Word Bank

Below is a list of words that you may use to illustrate words with beginning consonants. Some of these words are included in the Word/Picture Card set on pages 70–71. Ideas for using these cards and additional cards you may create yourself can be found in "Classroom Fun," pages 65–67.

Beginning Consonants

B	**D**	**G**	**J**	**M**	**P**	**R**	**T**	**X**
bag	deer	game	jacks	mail	paint	rain	tail	box
ball	desk	gas	jam	man	pan	rake	talk	fix
barn	dig	gate	jar	map	pat	rat	tape	fox
bat	dirt	gift	jeans	mat	pen	red	ten	mix
bed	dish	girl	jeep	match	pie	ring	tie	ox
bend	dive	go	jet	milk	pig	road	tip	six
bike	dog	goat	jog	mitten	pin	roll	toe	
bird	doll	golf	jug	moon	pour	rope	toy	**Y**
boy	door	goose	jump	mop	pull	rose	tub	yak
bug	down	gum		mouse	purse	rub		yam
bus	duck		**K**	mouth	push	run	**V**	yank
		H	key	mud			van	yard
C	**F**	hair	kid		**Qu**	**S**	vase	yawn
call	face	hand	kilt	**N**	quack	sail	vest	yarn
can	fall	hang	king	nail	quail	sand	vine	yellow
cap	fan	hat	kiss	neck	quart	sat	violin	yes
car	farm	head	kite	nest	queen	saw		yolk
cat	fence	hear		night	quilt	seven	**W**	
coat	fight	heart	**L**	nose		sing	wag	**Z**
comb	finger	hill	lamp	nurse		sink	wagon	zebra
cow	fire	hit	leaf	nut		six	walk	zig-zag
cut	fish	hole	leg			soap	watch	zipper
	five	hop	lick			sock	water	zoo
	foot	horn	line			soup	web	zoom
	four	house	lion			sun	wing	
	fox	hum	log				wink	
			look				wolf	

Short Vowels

Using This Book

Classroom Management

Reproducibles Reproducible pages 77–89 offer a variety of individual and partner activities. Answers to the activities are provided, as necessary, in the *Teacher Notes* section on page 100.

Directions You may wish to go over the directions with children and verify that they can identify all picture cues before they begin independent work.

Games When children play partner games, you may want to circulate to monitor that responses are correct and procedures have been understood.

Working with the Poem

A poem on page 76 introduces the phonics element in this book, short vowels. Start by reading this poem aloud to children. As children progress through the activities in this book, you may want to duplicate the poem so children can work with it in a variety of ways:

Echo Reading Recite the poem, line by line as a sing-song jump rope chant. Have children echo the words and rhythm.

Visual Discrimination Write the poem on a chart. Ask volunteers to underline the short vowels and circle the rhyming words.

Kinesthetic Activity Take children out to the playground and encourage them to jump rope while chanting the words to this poem.

Innovation Encourage children to work with a partner to think of other rhyming names. Have them use the names to make up new verses for the jump rope poem and perform the chant for the class.

Connecting School and Home

The Family Letter on page 75 can be sent home to encourage families to reinforce what children are learning. Children will also enjoy sharing the Take-Home Book on pages 91–92. You can cut and fold these booklets ahead of time, or invite children to participate in the process. You may also want to mount the pages on heavier stock so that you can place the Take-Home Book in your classroom library.

Picture Cards

Pages 98–99 of this book contain Word and Picture Cards drawn from the vocabulary presented in this book and other familiar daily vocabulary. You may wish to mount these cards on heavier stock as a classroom resource. You may also wish to duplicate and distribute them to children for use in matching and sorting activities. Each child can use a large envelope to store the cards.

Assessment

Page 90, Show What You Know, provides children with targeted practice in standardized test-taking skills, using the content presented in this book in the assessment items.

Dear Family,

In school your child is learning about short vowels.

hat

sun

You may enjoy sharing some or all of the following activities with your child.

Name Check
With your child, write down the names of family members, friends, and pets. Then have your child say each name aloud and identify the short vowel names with a checkmark.

Stand Up Categories
Choose a category. Slowly say the names of familiar items to your child. Have your child stand up when he or she hears a short vowel sound. Categories might include numbers *(six, ten)*, colors *(red, black)*, pets *(cat, dog, fish)*, or food *(fish, eggs, ham, jam)*.

Reading Together
To practice recognizing short vowels, go over your child's Take-Home Book, "Dot's Fun Sandwich." Ask your child to point out or circle the short vowels in the story.

You may also wish to look for the following books at your local library:

Inch by Inch
by Leo Lionni

Emma's Pet
by David McPhail

Sincerely,

Name _____

Best Friends

Danny and Manny
Rob and Bob
Jenny and Penny
Kim and Jim
Best friends, best friends, best friends all.
But who's the very best friend of all?
A - E - I - O - YOU!

Directions: Read the poem to the class once or twice just for fun. See page 74, "Working with the Poem," for more ideas.

Name _____

An A-1 Name Tag

Make a name tag for your desk.
Write your name on the line.

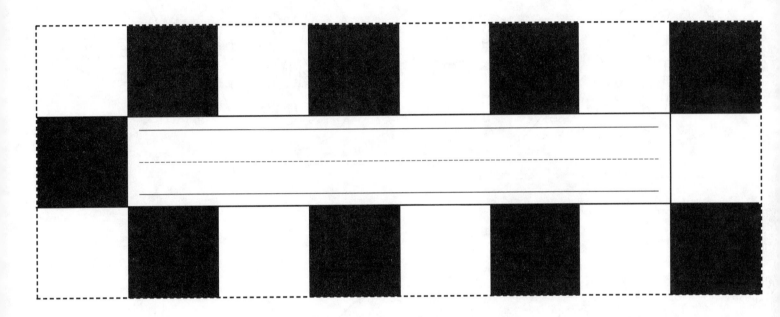

Directions: Tell children to write their names neatly on the line. Help children identify all the pictures (*ant, arrow, umbrella, alphabet, apple, anchor, flower, astronaut, ax, dog, inchworm, alligator*). Tell children they may decorate their name tags with pictures whose names begin with the short *a* sound. Have children cut and paste as many of the short *a* pictures as they like on to their name tags. Have children color the name tags, cut them out, and tape them on their desks.

Name _____

Extra Special Eggs

Color the extra special eggs.

  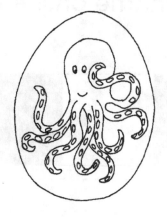 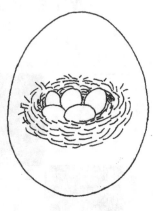

_____   _____   _____   _____

_____   _____   _____

Directions: Help the children identify the pictures in the egg shapes *(umbrella, elf, octopus, eggs, elbow, elephant, ant)*. Tell the children to say the name of each picture aloud, and then color in only the pictures whose names begin with the short *e* sound. Have children write *e* on the line below each picture they have colored in. Display children's Extra Special Eggs in the classroom.

Name _____

Izzy Inchworm

What should Izzy measure?

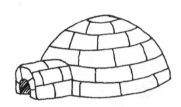

_____
- - - - - - - - - - -

_____
- - - - - - - - - - -

_____
- - - - - - - - - - -

_____
- - - - - - - - - - -

_____
- - - - - - - - - - -

_____
- - - - - - - - - - -

Directions: Tell children that Izzy Inchworm likes to measure things whose names begin like his, with the short *i* sound. Go over the picture names together (*igloo, iguana, insect, inchworm, umbrella, ink, elephant, apple*). After children identify the names of all the pictures, have them draw a line from Izzy to each picture whose name begins with the short *i* sound. Have children write the letter *i* on the line under each short *i* picture.

Name _____

Olive the Sea Serpent

Olive has some words to share.

_____   _____

Directions: Have children look at the letters on Olive the Sea Serpent. Encourage children to work with a partner to find three short words that begin with the short *o* sound. Then have each child circle the words and write them on the lines. As a bonus, have children look for Olive's name, circle it, and write it on the line.

Name _____

Under the Umbrella

It's raining! Get Uncle under the umbrella before he gets soaked!

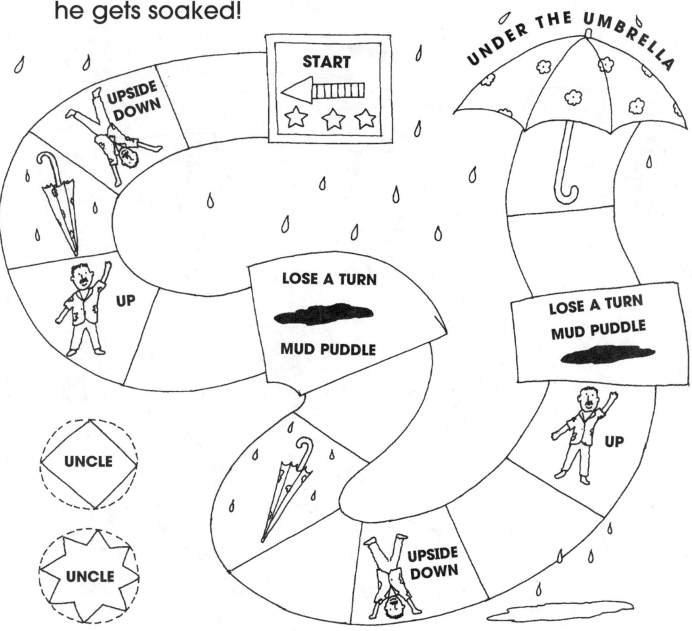

Directions: Children play this game in pairs. Have them cut out the UNCLE circles to use as playing pieces and place them on the START space. Then have children take turns tossing a number cube and moving their UNCLE circles that number of spaces. If the player lands on an UP box, he or she moves ahead an extra space. If the player lands on an UPSIDE DOWN box, he or she moves back one space. Landing on a folded umbrella space gives a player an extra turn. The first player to get UNCLE under the umbrella wins the game.

Follow the Path

Help Anteater get to the termite hill.

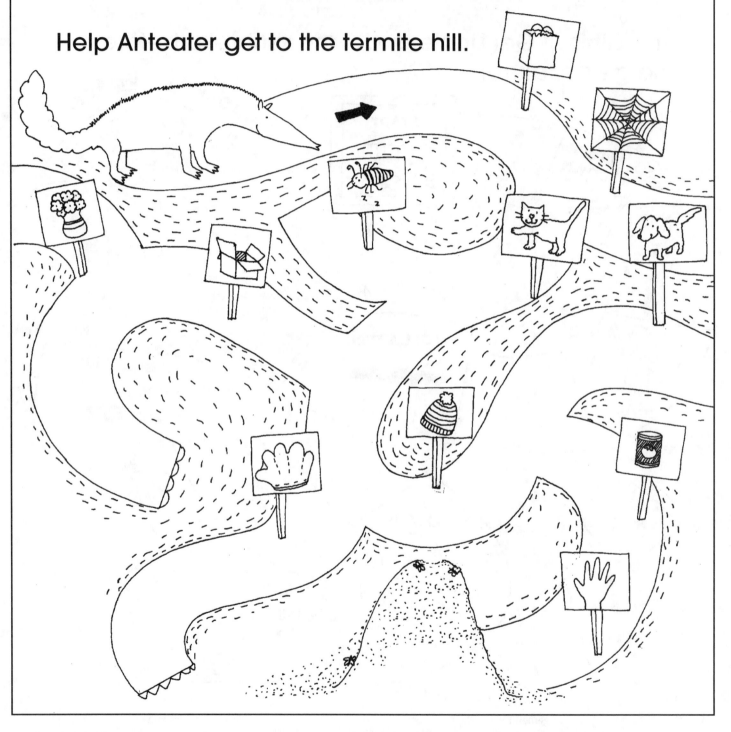

Directions: Explain to children that they will draw a line through the maze to show the Anteater the path to the termite hill. Tell children to follow the pictures whose names have the short *a* sound in them. Encourage children to work in pairs and to say all the picture names out loud.

Name _____

Find the Words

What is in the milk carton?

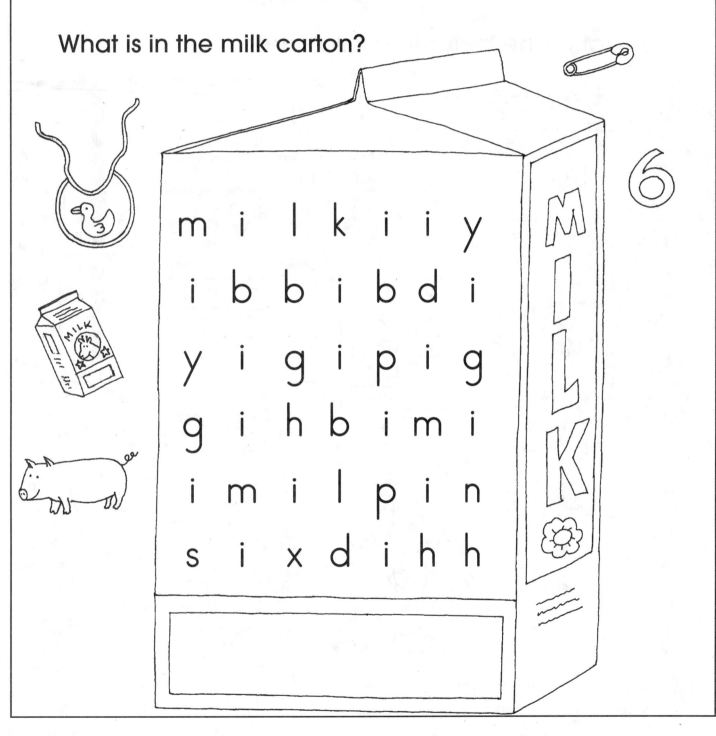

m	i	l	k	i	i	y
i	b	b	i	b	d	i
y	i	g	i	p	i	g
g	i	h	b	i	m	i
i	m	i	l	p	i	n
s	i	x	d	i	h	h

Directions: Have children look at the small pictures. Explain that children will find the names of these pictures hidden in the word search puzzle. Tell children to look at the letters in each row from left to right to find the short *i* names. Have children circle the words they find.

The Great Big Book of Fun Phonics Activities © Scholastic Professional Books

Name _____

Estella's Room

Look at all the things in Estella's room.

Directions: Tell children to look at Estella's room and say the name of each item in the room. When they find an item whose name has the short *e* sound, they should color it in. Encourage children to check with classmates if they are unsure of an item.

Name _____

Froggy's Hop

Help Froggy hop across the pond.

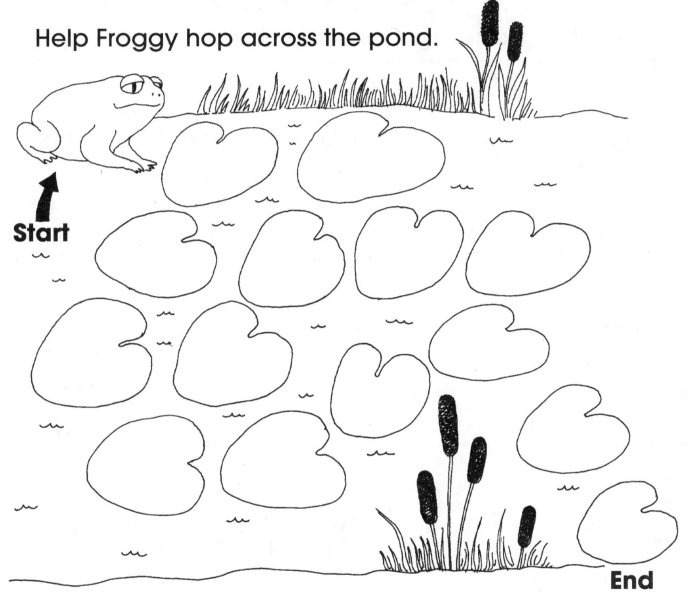

Start

End

Directions: Tell children they will help Froggy hop across the pond. They will cut out and paste pictures whose names have the short *o* sound on lily pads to make a path for Froggy. Children may choose to paste the pictures in any order as long as Froggy hops directly from one lily pad to another. Explain that children are not required to use up all the small pictures. Encourage volunteers to show their completed paths to the class and to "read" the picture names on their final paths aloud. Did every path turn out differently?

The Great Big Book of Fun Phonics Activities © Scholastic Professional Books

Name _____

What Is It?

Something is hiding. Can you find it?

jig	cat	bib	red	hot
bag	bug	rag	hug	hit
set	sun	sip	rut	kit
rib	rub	rug	up	lap
ten	tub	nut	jug	jog
mop	mud	bud	us	nap
mad	cub	mug	cup	pet

Directions: Tell children to look for words with the short *u* sound. Have them color in the whole box if it has a short *u* word. What is hiding there?

Name _____

Perfect Petals

Come to the garden. Make two perfect flowers.

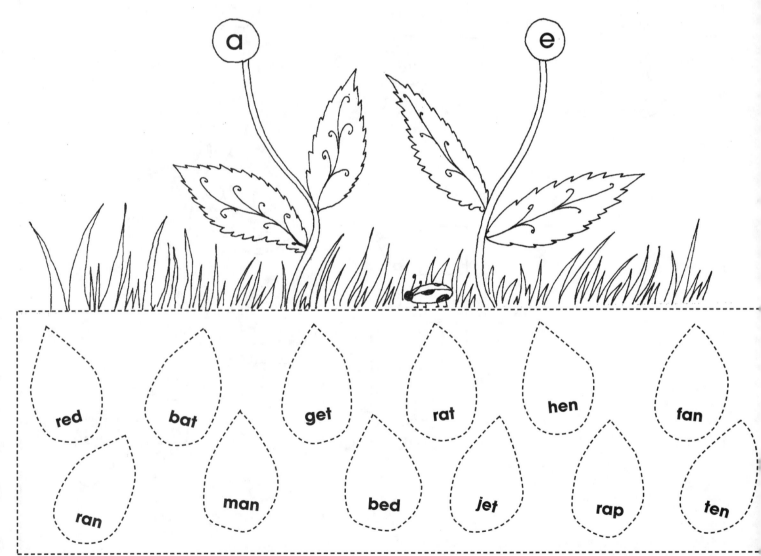

a

e

red   bat   get   rat   hen   fan

ran   man   bed   jet   rap   ten

Directions: Read all the words on the petals with the class before children complete the activity. Tell children to cut out the flower petals. They should paste the petals with short *a* words around the "a" flower and the petals with short *e* words around the "e" flower. Then have children color their flowers.

Name _____

Get Tug's Mail

Tug the Bug wants to get his mail. Help him climb down the steps.

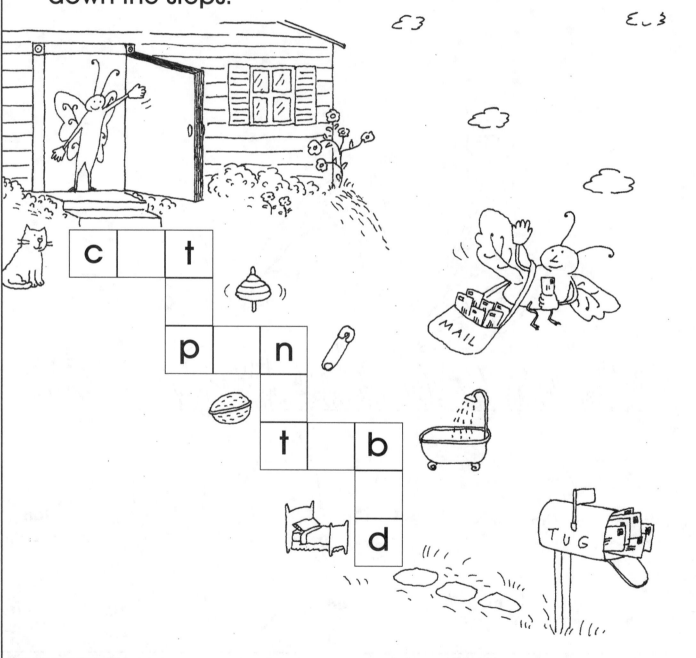

Directions: Children can complete the crossword puzzle individually or with partners. Go over the picture clues with the class first (*cat, top, pin, nut, tub, bed*).

The Great Big Book of Fun Phonics Activities © Scholastic Professional Books

Name _____

Calling All Words

How many words can you
call on the telephone?

1. c8p   cup

2. f2n

3. b4b

4. t3n

5. m6p

6. f6x

7. s2d

8. r3d

9. t8b

10. p4g

Directions: Tell children to "call up" these words. Have them find the vowel sound that is missing from each word by matching
the number in the word to the telephone code. Then have them write each word on the line.

Show What You Know

Say the name of each picture. Fill in the circle next to the letter that stands for the missing sound. Write the letter on the line.

1.	○ a ○ e ○ i ○ o ○ u	2.	○ a ○ e ○ i ○ o ○ u	3.	○ a ○ e ○ i ○ o ○ u
c _____ t		b _____ b		b _____ d	
4.	○ a ○ e ○ i ○ o ○ u	5.	○ a ○ e ○ i ○ o ○ u	6.	○ a ○ e ○ i ○ o ○ u
f _____ x		b _____ g		b _____ x	
7.	○ a ○ e ○ i ○ o ○ u	8.	○ a ○ e ○ i ○ o ○ u	9.	○ a ○ e ○ i ○ o ○ u
_____ gg		f _____ sh		h _____ t	

Directions: Go over the instructions with children, showing them how to fill in the circle and write the missing letter.

The Great Big Book of Fun Phonics Activities © Scholastic Professional Books

Now *this* is a FUN SANDWICH!

8

1

This is not fun yet.
I'll add a yummy cupcake.

6

This is not a fun sandwich.
I'll add a pickle.

3

I'm Dot.

This is my ham sandwich.

2

This is not really, really fun.
I'll add gum drops.

7

This is still not a fun sandwich.
I'll add a carrot.

4

This is not a fun sandwich yet.
I'll add an egg.

5

Classroom Fun ....

Short Vowels

Beanbag Vowel Toss

Organize children into two or three teams. Divide a big sheet of drawing paper into five sections. Write a vowel on each section. Then challenge children to a beanbag toss. Have team members take turns tossing the beanbag onto the paper. When the beanbag lands, have the child say the letter in that section and also think of a word that has that short vowel sound. Write the words on the chalkboard, keeping separate columns for each team. Players earn one point for each new word. The team with the most points at the end of the game wins.

Mystery Vowel

Choose a child who will be able to quickly recognize a particular short vowel sound. Quietly instruct the child to stand up, then sit again quickly every time he or she hears the vowel sound you have selected. Then read a story aloud slowly. The rest of the class will observe the volunteer standing and sitting as the story progresses. Ask the other children to raise their hands when they can guess what the mystery vowel is. When a number of hands have gone up, stop and let the class guess the short vowel.

What's My Word?

Work with the class to brainstorm words that have the short a sound in them. Write each word on an index card. Shuffle the index cards, and tape one word card to the front of each child's shirt. Each child must try to guess the word. Encourage children to go around the room, quietly asking questions about their words. Explain that they may only ask questions that can be answered by "Yes" or "No." For instance: *Is it an animal? No. Is it in the classroom? Yes. Does it have three letters? Yes. Does it start with b? Yes. Is it a "bag"? Yes!* Later, repeat the game using other short vowel words. Use the Word Bank on page 100 for ideas.

Vowel Collage

Divide the class into five groups and assign a short vowel to each group. Help the groups to brainstorm lots of words that use their assigned short vowel sound. Then have each group design and put together a collage that includes pictures of as many words as possible from the brainstorming list. Children may draw, paint, or cut and paste pictures from magazines. Label each collage and display all the collages in the classroom or elsewhere in the school.

Classroom Fun

Short Vowel Football

Draw a football field on the chalkboard, with a line marking every "10 yards." Draw a football on a sticky note and place it on the "50-yard line." Divide the class into two teams. Tell children that you will call out a vowel. You will challenge the first player to name a word that has the short sound of that vowel. If the player can name a word, he or she may move the "football" ten yards toward the goal. You will write the word on that team's side of the field. Then you will say another vowel for the player on the other team. If a team misses the answer, the other team gets a turn with the same vowel. Keep playing until there is a "touchdown."

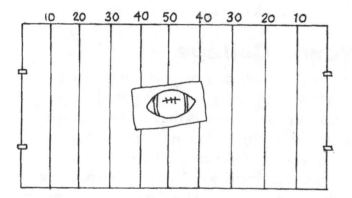

Short Vowel Day

Plan a Short Vowel Day. All the activities on that day must have names that contain short vowel sounds. For example, children may *run* or *hop*, but they may not *play games*! The names of all the snacks on Short Vowel Day should have short vowel sounds, too. Children can enjoy *milk* but not *juice*, use a *cup* but not a *plate*, and so on. Make up a poster celebrating the day. Invite other classes to join in with you, but be sure they understand the rules!

Play a Game of "It"

You will need a large open area. Set up two long parallel lines, about 10 yards apart, using cones or other markers. Line up all the children along one line. The child who volunteers to be "It" stands in the middle, between the two lines. Each player must silently think of a word that includes a short vowel. Then "It" names a vowel. If a player's word contains that vowel, he or she runs to the other line. "It " will try to tag as many players as possible as they run across. The players that "It" manages to tag must stay in the middle and help "It" catch more players when the next vowel is named. Eventually, all players will be in the middle and the game can begin again!

Word Strings

Go over the procedure carefully, and show children a completed word string before you begin. Divide the class into teams. Put both teams up at the board. Have the first player in each team write a consonant-vowel-consonant word(such as *cat*) on the board. The next player on each team then writes another C-V-C word that begins with the last letter of the previous word. A word string might look like this: *cat-top-pin-net-tub*. The first team to create a word string that includes all five vowels wins the game.

Play Short Vowel Bingo

Use the Short Vowel Bingo Pattern on page 97. Make copies of the page and hand them out to the class. Instruct the children to cut out the card and the pictures and to paste the pictures on the squares below the short vowel sound they match. Explain that children may paste the pictures for each column in any order they want. Give each child beans, pennies, or other small markers. Then play Short Vowel Bingo. At random, name a picture and the short vowel it matches. Children place their markers on the picture. The first player to fill a whole row, horizontally, vertically, or diagonally says "Bingo!" and wins the game.

Short Vowel Puppets

Brainstorm lots of names for puppet characters that begin with the short vowel *a, e, i, o,* and *u* sounds. Examples might be Annie Ant, Ed Elephant, Olive Orangutan, and Uncle Ugg. Talk about what all these characters might look like and act like. Encourage children to draw their favorites on paper plates and attach craft sticks to make stick puppets. Assign pairs to make up little dialogues that contain words with short vowel sounds and perform them for the class.

Telephone

Make up a sentence that uses lots of short vowel words. For example:

"Jack flapped his hand at the crab in the sand" or
"Jess left ten red eggs next to the nest."

Write the sentence on a piece of paper, but keep it to yourself. Have about six children sit in a row or in a circle. Whisper your sentence in the first child's ear and say, "Pass it on!" Each child whispers the sentence to the next. The last child in line should say the sentence he or she heard out loud. Then read what you wrote out loud to the children and see how the sentence has changed.

Hat Scrabble

Cut twenty index cards in half. On ten or so of the card pieces, write a consonant. On the other cards, write a phonogram, like *-et, -en, -ig,* or *-at.* Choose letter combinations that will create a variety of words with the consonant-short vowel-consonant pattern. The Word Bank on page 100 is a good source of ideas. Put all the card pieces in a hat or a paper bag and mix them up. Arrange children in teams, and have the first player on each team draw out two cards from the hat or bag. If a child draws a combination that makes a word, he or she can write it down on chart paper or the chalkboard. Then players put their cards back in the hat, shake it up, and the next player takes a turn. The team with the longest list of words after a given time limit wins the game.

Instant Activities

Hunt for Words Write a long word on the chalkboard. Challenge the class to find other shorter words within it and to list them on the board. For example the word *caterpillar* contains *cat, pit, tip, rip, rap, lip, pet* and more!

Ghost Vowels Have each child trace a short vowel on a partner's back. When the partner guesses the letter, he or she may turn and trace a letter on the first child's back.

Vowel Clubs Together with the class, make up rules for short vowel clubs. For example, only people with a short *a* sound in their names may be in the Short *a* Club. The Short *a* Club always meets in the *a*fternoon. Members have *a*pples and *a*pricots for snacks.

"Musical Cat" Have children stand in a circle and gently toss a toy cat or bat around while music plays. When you stop the music, the child holding the toy must say a word that has the short *a* sound. Vary the game by using a rubber duck for words with short *u*, a plastic fish for words with short *i*, and so on.

Play GO! Have all the children line up on one side of the room. You stand on the other side of the room and propose word riddles about words that begin with *a, e, i, o,* or *u*. For example, one riddle might be "My name begins with O and I have eight arms." Call on the first child who raises his or her hand. If he or she answers correctly, say "GO!" and allow the child to take a giant step. The first child to come close enough to tag you wins the game.

Vowel Art Assign a vowel to each child. Challenge children to quickly draw a picture in which their letter is hidden. Then have the children exchange pictures to find each other's vowel.

Short Vowel Pets Tell children to imagine the class will be getting a new cat, and it will need a short *a* name. Brainstorm cat names for just two minutes, but keep a sheet of chart paper available in the class so that children can add more names later. You might also brainstorm names for: a puppy (short *u*), a fish (short *i*), a hen (short *e*), and an octopus (short *o*).

Sandbox Vowels Keep a shallow box of sand on hand for children to practice writing their letters. Children can work in pairs, with one partner reading a short vowel word and the other child writing it in the sand.

Short Vowel Bingo Pattern

Aa	Ee	Ii	Oo	Uu

Word Cards

cat	hat	bag	bed
nest	hen	bib	fish
pig	fox	frog	sock
bug	jump	duck	hug

Picture Cards

Word Bank

Below is a list of words that you may use to illustrate words with short vowels. Some of these words are included in the Word/Picture Card set on pages 98–99. Ideas for using these cards and additional cards you may create yourself can be found in "Classroom Fun," pages 93–95.

Short Vowel Words

short a	short e	short i	short o	short u
ant	bed	bib	box	bug
back	bell	dig	clock	bunny
bad	bend	dish	dog	buzz
bag	desk	fish	dot	cub
bat	egg	gift	fox	cup
can	hen	hill	frog	duck
cat	jet	hit	hop	dust
catch	nest	igloo	mom	hug
fan	pet	ink	mop	hunt
grab	step	kick	ox	jug
has	ten	milk	pond	mud
hat	vest	pin	rock	nut
man	web	sip	sock	rub
pan		skip	stop	rug
pat		ship		skunk
sad		wink		sun
van				tub
				us
				up

Teacher Notes

Page 77 *Answers:* Children may choose ant, arrow, alphabet, apple, anchor, astronaut, ax, or alligator.

Page 78 *Answers:* elephant, elbow, egg, elf.

Page 79 *Answers:* igloo, inchworm, iguana.

Page 80 *Answers:* on, off, ox; *bonus*—Olive.

Page 82 *Answers:* bag, cat, hat, can, hand.

Page 83 *Answers:* bib, milk, pig, pin, six.

Page 84 *Answers:* bed, desk, pencils, Estella sign, Estella T-shirt, pegs, dress, shelf, elephant, elf, sled, shell, hen, jet.

Page 86 *Answer:* A bunny.

Page 87 *Answers:* "a" flower—bat, rat, fan, ran, man, rap; "e" flower—red, get, hen, bed, jet, ten.

Page 88 *Answers:* cat, top, pin, nut, bed.

Page 89 *Answers:* cup, fan, bib, ten, mop, fox, sad, red, tub, pig.

Rhyming Words

Using This Book

Classroom Management

Reproducibles Reproducible pages 105–117 offer a variety of individual and partner activities. Answers appear as necessary in the *Teacher Notes* section on page 128.

Directions You may want to go over the directions with children and verify that they can identify all picture cues before they begin any independent work.

Games When children play partner games, you may want to circulate to make sure that the children understand the procedures.

Working with the Poem

A poem on page 104 introduces the phonics element in this book, rhyming words. Start by reading this poem aloud to children. As children progress through the activities in this book, you may want to duplicate the poem so children can work with it in a variety of ways:

Personal Response Read the poem aloud. Ask children to tell about their own baby sisters or brothers, and to share any "surprises" they have had.

Echo Reading Recite the poem, line by line. Have children echo the words and rhythm.

Visual Discrimination Write the poem on a chart. Ask volunteers to circle the rhyming words.

Innovation Encourage children to tell you how the poem would have changed if it were about a baby brother. Write the revised poem on a chart and then recite it together.

Connecting School and Home

The Family Letter on page 103 can be sent home to encourage families to reinforce what children are learning. Children will also enjoy sharing the Take-Home Book on pages 119–120. You can cut and fold these booklets ahead of time, or invite children to participate in the process. You might also mount the pages on heavier stock so you can place the Take-Home Book in your classroom library.

Picture Cards

Pages 126–127 of this book contain Word and Picture Cards drawn from the vocabulary presented in this book and other familiar daily vocabulary. You may wish to mount these cards on heavier stock as a classroom resource. You may also wish to duplicate and distribute them to children for use in matching and sorting activities. Each child can use a large envelope to store the cards.

Assessment

Page 118, Show What You Know, provides children with targeted practice in standardized test-taking skills, using the content presented in this book in the assessment items.

Dear Family,

Your child is learning in school about rhyming words.

b**at**   c**at**   h**at**

You may enjoy sharing some or all of the following activities with your child.

Change a Letter

You can use any surface for writing — paper, a small chalkboard, or even a tray of sand — to practice making new words with phonograms. Write a word like *cat* and erase the *c*. Have your child write another consonant letter to make a new word. Check to be sure the new word is real, not a nonsense word.

Rhyme Time

Tell your child that every so often you will surprise him or her by saying "It's rhyme time." Ask your child to look around for an object or printed word nearby, and then say that word and another word that rhymes with it.

Reading Together

To practice recognizing rhyming words, go over your child's Take-Home Book, "Dinosaurs." Ask your child to point out or circle the rhyming words in the story.

You may also wish to look for the following books at your local library:

Sincerely,

Pierre

by Maurice Sendak

Green Eggs and Ham

by Dr. Seuss

Name _____

My Baby Sister

I have a baby sister.
She came not long ago.
I thought I'd go into her room,
Just to say hello.
I thought I'd try to hug her
And kiss her on the cheeks.
What a big surprise I got—
My baby sister leaks!

Directions: Read the poem to the class once or twice just for fun. See page 102, "Working with the Poem," for more ideas.

Name _____

Flip Out!

You can make your own flip book.

jet

net

pet

wet

et

Directions: Go over the names of the pictures on this page. Tell children to write the beginning letter for each picture and to color the pictures. Ask them what all the words have in common. (They rhyme.) Then help them assemble a flip book. Have children cut out the pages and place the strip for the phonogram *et* on the bottom. Have children lay the four picture pages on top of the *et* strip. Staple the pages in the upper left corner. Encourage children to flip through the pages and read the words.

Name _____

Roll-A-Rhyme

Get ready to rock
and rhyme!

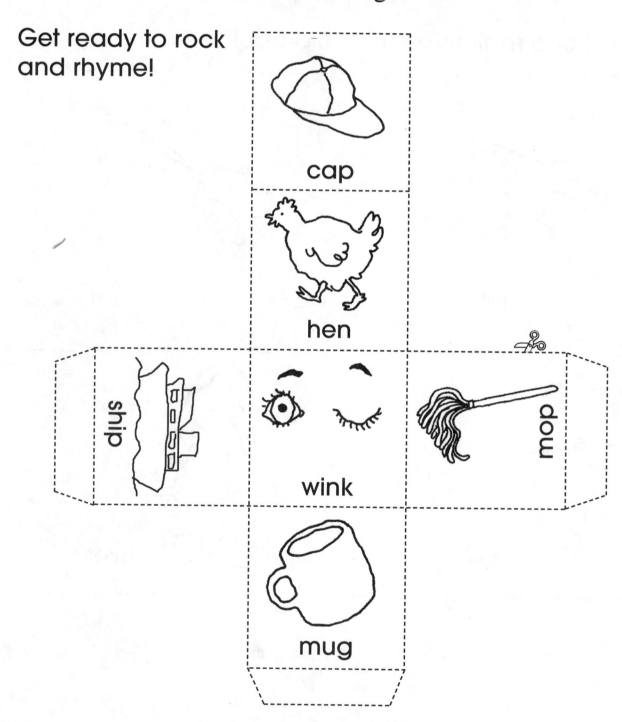

cap

hen

ship

wink

mop

mug

Directions: Help children construct the rhyme cube. Glue or paste the page to lightweight cardboard and cut out the cube. Fold it and tape it together. Suggest games children can play with the cube in pairs. For example, they can take turns rolling it and saying a rhyme that matches the picture and word on top, one point per rhyme. Or they can roll it, then work as teams to think of as many rhyming words as possible. Encourage children to keep or dictate a list of their rhyming words.

Name _____

How Puzzling!

Match up the rhyming words and see what you get!

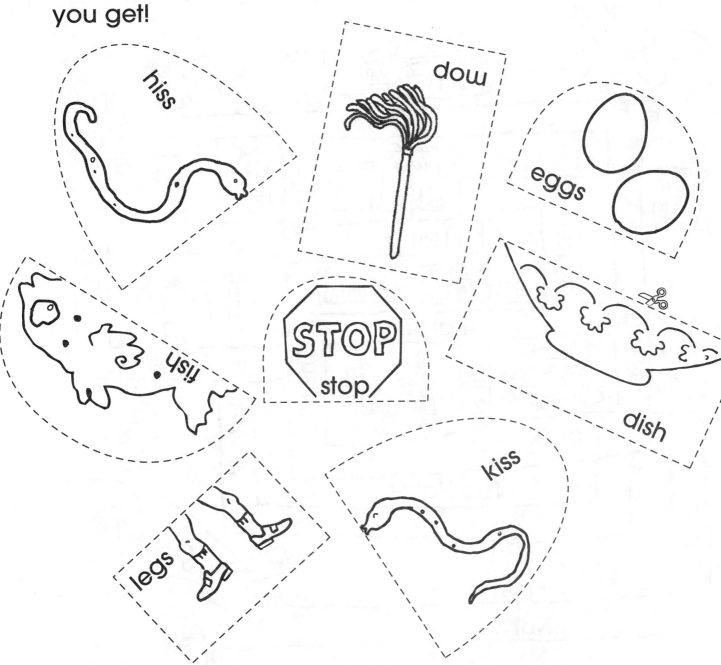

hiss

dow

eggs

fish

STOP
stop

dish

legs

kiss

Directions: Tell children to cut out the puzzle pieces. Explain that the idea is to find pairs of puzzle pieces with rhyming names. When they find a match, children should tape the two pieces together to create a silly picture. After children complete the page, they can use words from the Word Bank on page 29 to make their own rhyming puzzles.

Scat, Billy Bat!

Billy Bat is lost in the city. Help him get home to his cave.

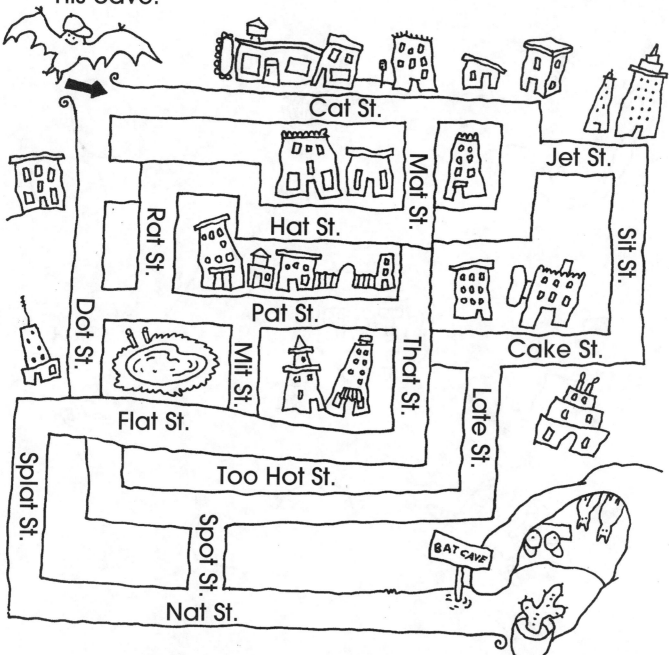

Directions: Explain to children that they will help Billy Bat find his way through the maze of streets to get home to the bat cave. If children follow streets whose names rhyme with *bat,* they will find their way. When children have completed the maze, they can read the names of the streets they followed aloud.

Name _____

Book Looks

These bookmarks will help you **look** in your **book!**

Directions: Have children cut out the small pictures and paste each one on the bookmark with a rhyming picture at the top. Then children can color the pictures and cut out the bookmarks. You may want to have children paste the paper bookmarks onto lightweight cardboard for greater durability. Encourage children to use the bookmarks in school and to take one home to use with library books.

Find-A-Rhyme

Help Bub the cub!
He has dropped
his rhyming words
in the tub.

s	l	s	u	h	u	l	c	u	b
s	u	n	h	b	u	n	g	u	b
n	u	h	t	u	b	l	u	n	d
g	r	s	b	u	u	n	f	u	n

Directions: Read the direction line with children. Tell them to look in the tub for two words that rhyme with *Bub* and two words that rhyme with *run*. One extra word (*sun*) is circled for them as an example. Children will read left to right to find all the words and write the words on the lines. After children complete the page, they might like to make up their own rhyming word searches and exchange papers with a partner. Have the partners circle each other's hidden words.

Name _____

Yes or No?

Read the questions. Write **yes** or **no** on the lines.

_____

1. Can a be on a  ? _____

2. Can a  drive a  ? _____

3. Can a really 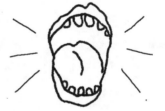 ? _____

4. Can a  really  ? _____

5. Can a   see a   ? _____

Directions: Go over the rhyming questions with the class. Make sure children understand the meaning of the pictures. Then have children write *yes* or *no* on the lines to answer each question. Encourage children to work with a partner to make up their own *yes* or *no* rhyming question in the last item.

Name _____

Puppet Time

You can make a puppet!

Sad Brad
Swell Nell
Lucky Chucky

Sad Brad

Directions: Tell children they will make a stick puppet with a rhyming name. They should draw a character inside the dashed art space. Then they will choose a rhyming name for their puppet. Children may choose a name from the word box or make up one of their own. They should assemble the puppet, pasting the character to one craft stick and the label to another, then pasting or taping them together. With partners, children can make up little rhyming skits to act out with their puppets for the class.

Rhyming Words **-ad, -ell, -im, -ug, -ucky, -ed**

Name _____

Pick a Pocket

Place words in your pocket chart.

-am
-end
-ick
-og
-um

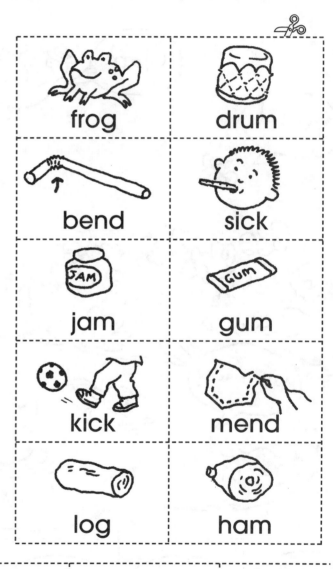

frog   drum

bend   sick

jam   gum

kick   mend

log   ham

-am	-end	-ick	-og	-um

Directions Read the endings and the words on the page with the children. Tell children to cut out the boxes with endings from the bottom of the page. Have them match each ending to one of the pockets on the pocket chart. Tell children to paste each ending in place with a thin strip of paste at the bottom, leaving the top of the label unpasted. Finally, have children cut out the word cards, sort them by endings, and place each one in the correct pocket of the chart.

Rhyming Words **-am, -end, -ick, -og, -um**

Name _____

What Did They Say?

What is going on at the pond?

Directions: Look over the scene with children. Read or have volunteers read the speech balloons. Point out that the animals are not making sense. Tell children to cut out the word balloons from the bottom of the page and paste each one in the scene over the word it rhymes with. When children have reassembled the scene, have them take turns acting out what the animals are really saying.

Rhyming Words -ap, -im, -ack, -uzz, -op, -ulp

Name _____

Daps Without Caps

Help the Daps. They need new caps.

These Daps need caps.
Do you know why?
Ten thousand mosquitoes
Are flying by.
Daps have three feet
But not one hand.
What will they do
When mosquitoes land?

> **Cap Ideas**
> A Cap Trap
> A Flap Cap
> The Slap Cap

Write the name of your cap. How does it work?

_____

_____

_____

_____

Directions: Read the poem aloud. Talk about why the Daps need caps. (Daps need caps because they have no hands to smack the mosquitoes.) Tell children they may work together to create special caps for the Daps. Discuss the caps named in the box. Ask children how they think each one would work and what it would look like. Then have children think about new caps for the Daps. Encourage children to write or dictate their cap descriptions.

Hink Pinks

Have fun with these word riddles.

What do you call two smiles?

What do you call a doggy kiss?

What do you call a silly rabbit?

What do you call a fast sweeper?

funny	grin	smooch	broom
zoom	pooch	twin	bunny

Directions: Help children understand the concept of rhyming Hink Pinks by giving a few examples: A chubby mouse is a *fat rat*. A mallard with money is a *lucky ducky*. Ice cream is a *sweet treat*. Help children read the questions and then have them cut out the words at the bottom and paste them where they belong to answer the questions with Hink Pinks. Encourage children to work together to invent more Hink Pinks.

Name _____

Who's Out Walking?

Connect the dots to find out who is out walking.

Directions Look over the page with children, asking volunteers to read words aloud. Then ask children to draw lines to connect pairs of rhyming words. You may want to encourage pairs of children to work together to identify the rhymes. Ask children to answer the title question, "Who's Out Walking?" Then have children color the scene.

Name _____

Show What You Know

Say the name of each picture. Fill in the circle next to the word that rhymes.

1.
   ○ big
   ○ cat
   ○ bet

2.
   ○ set
   ○ bat
   ○ new

3.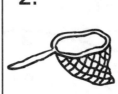
   ○ rip
   ○ lap
   ○ can

4.
   ○ jet
   ○ jump
   ○ hug

5.
   ○ sink
   ○ wet
   ○ wing

6.
   ○ flag
   ○ vest
   ○ fan

7.
   ○ best
   ○ well
   ○ bit

8.
   ○ dish
   ○ fit
   ○ fizz

9.
   ○ rip
   ○ king
   ○ rest

Directions: Go over the instructions with children, showing them how to fill in the circles.

1

What made them disappear?

8

Dinosaurs were here.

6

Dinosaurs scratched.

3

Dinosaurs hatched.

2

7

Dinosaurs chomped.

4

Dinosaurs stomped.

5

Classroom Fun ...

Rhyming Words

Rhyme Guy

Cut out the Rhyme Guy character from page 125 and mount it on a stiff piece a cardboard, folding back the bottom so that it can stand. Cut the slits in the Rhyme Guy's hands as shown. Place a strip of paper through the slits to display a word or a rhyming pair. As much as possible, display the Rhyme Guy and make him part of your classroom routine as you study rhyming words. For example, you can place a "word of the day" in Rhyme Guy's hands. Children can write down rhyming words throughout class and share them at the end of the day. More ideas for using Rhyme Guy appear in other Classroom Fun activities.

Stand Up, Sit Down

Assign a word to one child in the class. Make sure it ends in a very common phonogram, like *-at* or *-an*. Instruct the child to stand up, then sit again quickly and quietly when he or she hears the word or a word that rhymes with it. Then read a story or poem aloud slowly. Ask the other children to raise their hands when they think they can guess what the mystery sound is. When a number of hands go up, stop and let the class guess the sound.

Whisper Clues

Write some very common words on index cards, one word to a card. Mix the cards up and tape one word on each child's back. Tell children to walk around the room and quietly share clues. They will read a word on a classmate's back, and then whisper in his or her ear a rhyming word as a clue. A child may guess by whispering back what he or she thinks the target word is. If correct, that child may sit down. Continue until every child is sitting. Then invite each child to stand and say the word aloud, along with as many of the rhyming clues as he or she can remember.

Write a Song

It can be lots of fun to write new lyrics for familiar songs, and it's good rhyming practice, too. Make it a fun class project once or twice, and soon children will be doing it on their own! Start with a song like "I'm a Little Teapot" or "Twinkle, Twinkle Little Star." Here is one example.

Twinkle, twinkle, little mouse.
Why are you here in my house?
Up inside my walls so stout.
How will I ever get you out?
Twinkle, twinkle, little mouse.
Why are you inside my house?

Classroom Fun

Class Poets

Encourage children to collaborate with one another to write their own poems. You may want to post some of the rhyming words from the Word Bank on page 128 on a bulletin board. You might also provide rhyming frames to help children get started. For example,

> Star [light]
> Star [bright]
> First star
> [I see tonight.]

In your frame you could leave out the rhyming words. Children could make a new version of this poem:

> Star *new*
> Star *old*
> First star
> *Looks so cold.*

Encourage children to perform their poems for the class. Display the poems or compile a class poetry book.

> Star _____
> Star _____
> First star
>
> _____

Hop-Scotch Rhymes

Almost any game can become a rhyming game. Do your students like to play Hopscotch at recess? Make it a rhyme challenge game by writing a word in each Hopscotch box. The rules of the game are exactly the same, except that players have to say a rhyming word before picking up the stone and hopping home. Think about the other games your class plays every day. Can you spice them up with rhymes?

Poem Shapes

Choose a word family that you have been studying or one from the Word Bank on page 128. Find a word in the family that suggests a definite shape. For example, there are a number of words that rhyme with *sun*. Draw a large simple sun on chart paper, and ask children to dictate short poems that you will write inside the sun. Encourage children to copy the poem shape to take home.

Rhyme Relay Race

Divide the class into three or four teams and have each team line up. On the board, write a word for each team. The words can be chosen from the Word Bank; choose words that are easy to rhyme. In turn, each child in line must go up to the board and write a rhyming word under his or her team's word, then move to the end of the line. Team members may help one another think of words. The game ends when teams run out of rhyming words.

Team A	Team B	Team C
did	fun	had
hid	run	dad
bid	sun	

"Go Fish-Dish-Wish"

Make up a set of about 36 playing cards, using many different rhyming pairs. (You may want to purchase a blank set of cards or laminate cardboard for durability.) Tell children they will use the cards to play "Go Fish-Dish-Wish." The rules are similar to those for the traditional game. The only difference is children will be looking for matching rhyming words.

DO YOU HAVE A WORD THAT RHYMES WITH FAN?

Rhyming Scrabble

Using index cards, create about ten phonogram strips that are roughly the same height as the tiles in Scrabble. Place the phonogram strips face down along with a set of regular Scrabble tiles. Children take turns making words on the table top, using either the regular tiles or tiles and the squares. Rules of the game are the same as Scrabble except for this — if one child makes a word like *cat*, using the paper *-at*, another player can make another word by putting a tile over the *c*, to make a rhyming word. You may want to simplify scoring, having children score one point for each word they make, two points for a word that rhymes with any other word on the board.

Rhyme Race

Prepare for this activity by placing a word in the arms of the Rhyme Guy (pattern found on page 125). Hold a rhyming race. Who can be the first to think of four words that rhyme with *cat*? Have children write their words and then raise their hands to present the words to the class. You can also combine this game with an activity on following directions. The directions can vary. For example, you might say, "Who can think of three words that rhyme with *sad*, write them on the board, turn around three times, and run back to sit down?"

Beanbag Rhyme Toss

Organize children into two or three teams. Divide a big sheet of drawing paper into five sections. Write a word on each section. Then challenge children to a beanbag toss. Have team members take turns tossing the beanbag onto the paper. When the beanbag lands, have the child say the word in that section and also think of a rhyming word. Write the words on the chalkboard, keeping separate columns for each team. Players earn one point for each new word. The team with the most points at the end of the game wins.

Instant Activities

Bean Bag Rhymes Have children stand in a circle and toss a bean bag around. Start them off with a word that is easy to rhyme. Have the child holding the bean bag say a rhyming word and then toss the bean bag to the next person. If the child can not think of a rhyming word, he or she may say "pass" and hand, not toss, the beanbag to the next child. After three children in a row say "pass," start a new word.

Riddle Rhymes Make up riddles for a number of words that rhyme. Encourage children to call out the rhyming answer. For example, say, "All these words rhyme with *hug*."

> I am an insect; you call me a _____.
> *(bug)*
> You walk on me; you call me
> a _____. *(rug)*
> You put hot drinks in me; you call
> me a _____. *(mug)*

Clap and Stamp Read lots of poems and rhyming books. (Some well-known poetry authors include Shel Silverstein, Jack Prelutsky, and Bruce Lansky.) As you read from poetry books, encourage the children to chant the rhyming words and to clap and stamp so that the poem is accompanied by a whole percussion band.

Rhyme Challenge Make up some quick rhymes and say them out loud, leaving off the last word. Encourage the class to call out the rhyming word together. When necessary, give a little clue. For example, if the last word is "shoe," you can lift up your foot.

> *Look!* I have a _____. *(book)*
> I think there's *glue* on my _____.
> *(shoe)*

GO! Have all the children line up on one side of the room. You stand on the other side of the room and call out a word. Children must think of two words that rhyme with that word. When children know the answer, they raise their hands. Call on the first child who raises his or her hand. If he or she answers correctly, shout 'GO!' and allow the child to take a giant step. The first child to tag you wins the game.

"I Spy" Rhymes Play a rhyming version of "I Spy," using items in the classroom. For example, "I spy something that rhymes with *look*." *(book)* Or, "I spy something that rhymes with *moo*." *(shoe)*

Rhyme Guy Pattern

Word Cards

bag	flag	cat	hat
bed	sled	hen	ten
pig	dig	sock	clock
frog	dog	bug	rug

Picture Cards

Word Bank

Below is a list of words that you may use to illustrate rhyming words. Some of these words are included in the Word/Picture Card set on pages 126–127. Ideas for using these cards and additional cards you may create yourself can be found in "Classroom Fun," pages 121–123.

─── **Rhyming Words** ───

ag	**-at**	**-est**	**-ill**	**-ock**	**-ot**	**-unk**
bag	bat	best	bill	block	hot	bunk
flag	cat	nest	hill	clock	not	junk
tag	fat	rest	mill	knock	pot	skunk
wag	hat	test	will	lock	spot	trunk
	mat			rock		
-an	pat	**-et**	**-in**	sock	**-ug**	
can	sat	bet	bin		bug	
fan		get	fin	**-og**	hug	
man	**-ed**	jet	pin	dog	mug	
pan	bed	net	win	frog	rug	
ran	fed	pet	grin	jog		
van	red	wet		log	**-um**	
	sled		**-ip**		hum	
-ap		**ig**	dip	**-op**	drum	
cap	**-en**	big	hip	hop		
lap	hen	dig	lip	mop	**-ump**	
map	men	pig	sip	pop	bump	
nap	pen	wig	trip	stop	jump	
tap	ten			top		

Teacher Notes

Page 105 *Answers:* jet, net, pet, wet.

Page 107 *Answers:* fish/dish, eggs/legs, mop/stop, hiss/kiss.

Page 108 *Answers:* Billy Bat will go through Cat St., Mat St., Hat St., Rat St., Pat St., That St., Flat St., Splat St., Nat St.

Page 109 *Answers:* King—swing, ring, wing; Fan—can, pan, van; Bug—hug, rug, mug.

Page 110 *Answers:* Bub—cub, tub; run—fun, bun.

Page 111 *Answers:* 1. yes 2. no 3. no 4. yes.

Page 113 *Answers:* am—ham, jam; end—bend, send; kick—quick, click; dog—log, jog; gum—hum, drum

Page 114 *Answers:* Clap!—Flap!, Fuzz!—Buzz!, POP—HOP, Rulp—Gulp: Him!—Swim!, Mack-mack!— Quack-quack!

Page 116 *Answers:* twin grin; pooch smooch; funny bunny; zoom broom.

Page 118 *Answers:* 1. cat 2. set 3. lap 4. hug 5. sink 6. fan 7. well 8. dish 9. king.

Beginning & Ending Consonants

Using This Book

Classroom Management

Reproducibles Reproducible pages 133–145 offer a variety of individual and partner activities. Simple directions to the children are augmented when necessary by *Answers* or *Game Directions* in the *Teacher Notes* section on page 156.

Directions You may wish to go over the directions with children and verify that they can identify all picture cues before they begin independent work.

Games When children play partner games, you may want to circulate in order to monitor that responses are correct and procedures have been understood.

Working with the Poem

A poem on page 132 introduces the phonics elements in this book, beginning and ending consonants. Start by reading this page aloud to children. Duplicate the poem so children can work with it in a variety of ways:

Personal Response Read the poem aloud and have children talk about it. Ask if the poem made them laugh.

Phonemic Awareness Read the poem aloud each day. Ask children to listen for a particular beginning or ending consonant sound and to raise their hands when they hear it.

Sound to Letter Write the poem on a chart, and ask children to point to or circle words that begin or end with a particular consonant sound.

Innovation Ask children to brainstorm ideas first. Then duplicate one line or more of the poem, leaving a blank. Encourage children to "write" an original verse by filling in the blank.

Connecting School and Home

The Family Letter on page 131 can be sent home to encourage families to reinforce what children are learning. Children will also enjoy sharing the Take-Home Book on pages 147–148. You can cut and fold these booklets ahead of time, or invite children to participate in the process. You may also mount the pages on heavier stock so you can place the Take-Home Book in your classroom library.

Word Card Sets

Pages 154–155 of this book contain matching sets of Word and Picture Cards drawn from the vocabulary presented in this book. You may wish to mount these on heavier stock as a classroom resource. You may also wish to duplicate and distribute them to children for use in matching and sorting activities. Each child can use a large envelope to store the cards.

Assessment

Page 146, Show What You Know, provides children with targeted practice in standardized test-taking skills, using the content presented in this book in the assessment items.

Dear Family,

Your child is learning in school about the beginning and ending sounds of consonants.

Beginning Consonant

t...

Ending Consonant

...k

You may enjoy sharing some or all of the following activities with your child:

Grocery Store Search

As you shop for groceries, name a consonant letter. Ask your child to point to an item whose name begins or ends with that letter sound.

Car Trip Hunt

On a car trip, challenge your child to name a letter that can be seen on a sign or license plate. Ask your child to think of a word that begins or ends with the sound of that letter.

Reading Together

To practice reading words with beginning and ending consonants, look over your child's Take-Home Book, "Good Job!" Point to pictures in the book. Ask your child to say the name of the picture and give the beginning or ending sounds.

You may also wish to look for these books in your local library:

Sincerely,

Dad's Dinosaur Day
by Diane Dawson Hearn

Noisy Nora
by Rosemary Wells

Fun in a Tub

Fox and Cub
Had fun in a tub
Full of water to the very top.
But jump! zoom! dip!
The tub began to tip.
Yes! Quick! Go get a mop!

Name _____

Balloon Fun

Color the pictures whose names **begin** with the letter on the animal's T-shirt: **b, m,** or **t.**

Name _____

On the Farm

Look at the scene. Find pictures whose names **begin** with **f, g,** or **j**. Write the correct letter on the line. Then color the scene.

Match It!

Say the names of the two big pictures, **desk** and **pumpkin**. Read the names of the small pictures. Cut them out. Paste the pictures whose names begin with **d** on the **desk**. Paste the pictures whose names begin with **p** in the **pumpkin**.

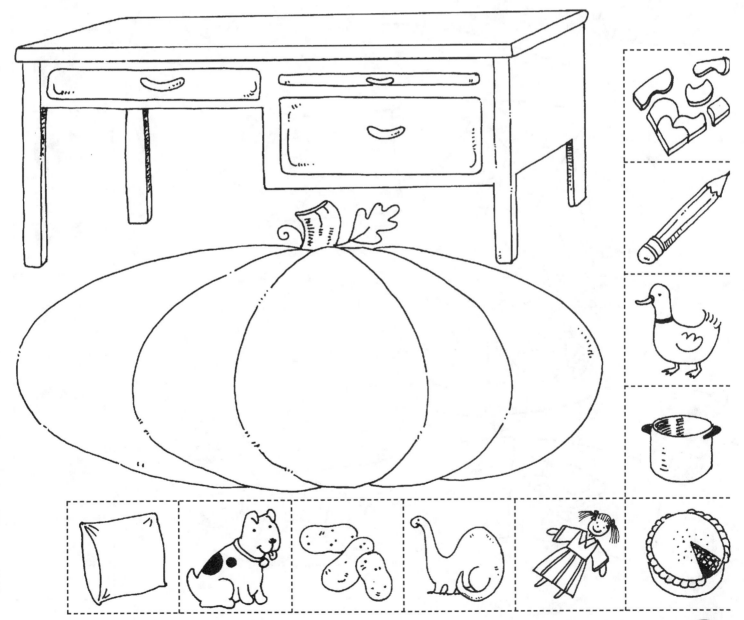

Name _____

Mother, Where Are You?

Help the lion cub find its mother. Your teacher will tell you how to play this game.

Beginning Consonants s, l, r

Name _____

What Is Hiding?

Look at the scene. Color in red each picture whose name begins with **h**. Color in blue each picture whose name begins with **w**. Find the three hidden **v** pictures. Circle them.

HOTEL

HOTEL

Name _____

Mixed-Up Kites

It's a windy day. The kites got mixed up. Trace each kite string from the letter to the picture whose name starts with that letter. Then color the **k** pictures **green** and the **n** pictures **yellow**.

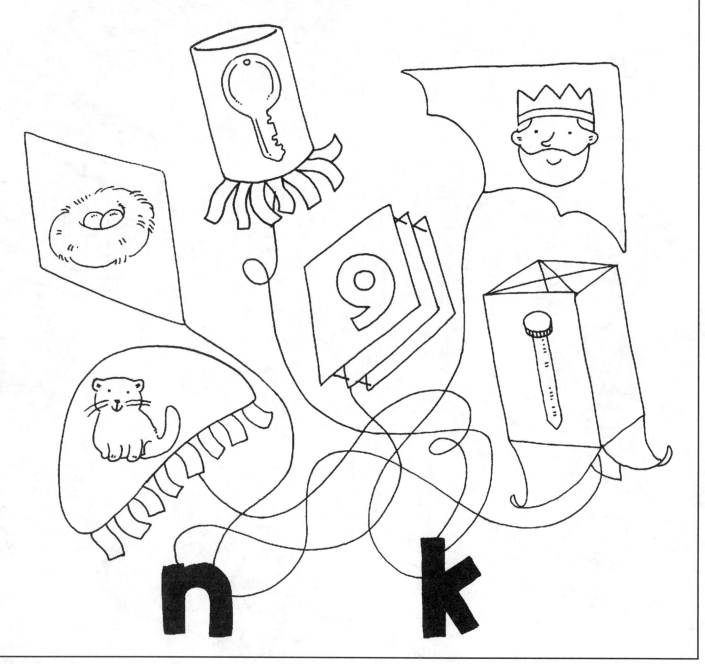

Name _____

Pack the Backpacks

Help Quinn, Yolanda, and Zoe pack their backpacks.
Cut out the pictures below.
Say the name of each picture.
Paste **q** pictures in Quinn's backpack.
Paste **y** pictures in Yolanda's backpack.
Paste **z** pictures in Zoe's backpack.

Animal Puzzles

Listen for the beginning sound of each animal's name. Find the letter that stands for that sound. Cut and paste the puzzle piece where it belongs.

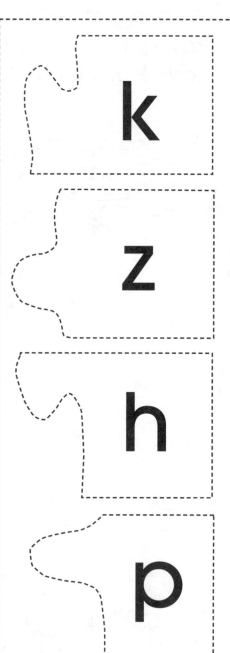

Reviewing Beginning Consonants **k, z, p, h**

Name _____

Picture Perfect

Matt drew two pictures whose names **end** in **t**. Paste them here.

Ann drew two pictures whose names **end** in **n**. Paste them here.

Meg drew two pictures whose names **end** in **g**. Paste them here.

Draw a picture that belongs in the last box of each row.

Name _____

Finish Line

Help the racers win the race. Your teacher will tell you how to play the game.

1
2
1
2
1
2
1
2

Ending Consonants **m, b, f**

Name _____

Find Baby Fox

Help the fox find its baby in the maze.
Follow pictures on the path whose names **end**
in the sounds of **x, v,** and **r.**

Start

Name _____

Raise the Flags!

It's time to raise the flags! Listen to the ending sound
of each picture name.

Color the **s** picture
flags **orange**.

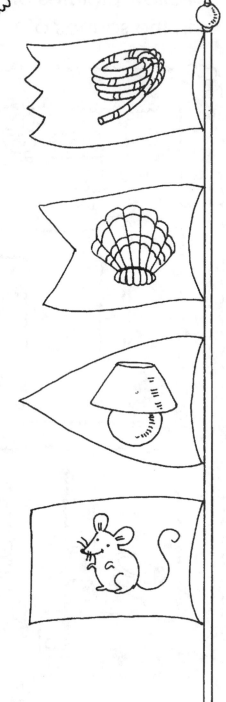

Color the **l** picture
flags **purple**.

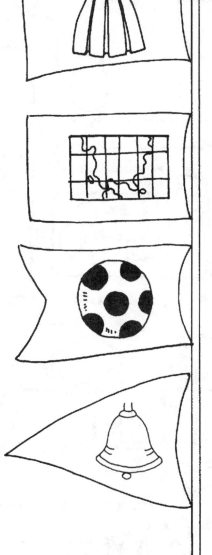

Color the **p** picture
flags **green**.

Name _____

Picture Dominoes

Cut out the pictures below. Then play dominoes
by matching the pictures whose names have the
same ending sound. Make new picture dominoes
by cutting out pictures from magazines.

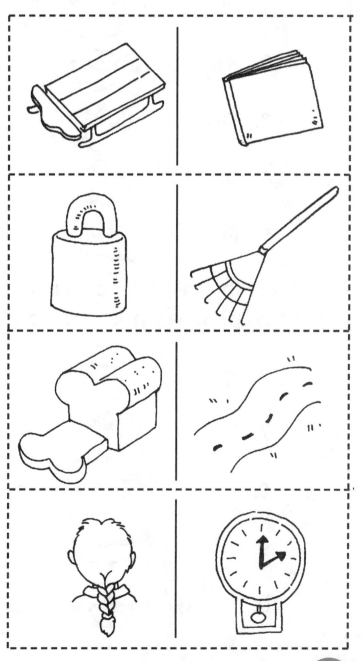

Show What You Know

Practice taking tests. Read the letter in each row. Fill in the circle next to each picture whose name **begins** with that sound.

1. **Pp**
2. **Nn**
3. **Qq**
4. **Dd**
5. **Ff**

Read the letter in each row. Fill in the circle next to each picture whose name **ends** with that sound.

6. **g**
7. **k**
8. **s**
9. **t**
10. **l**

Standardized Test-Taking Skills: *Beginning & Ending Consonants*

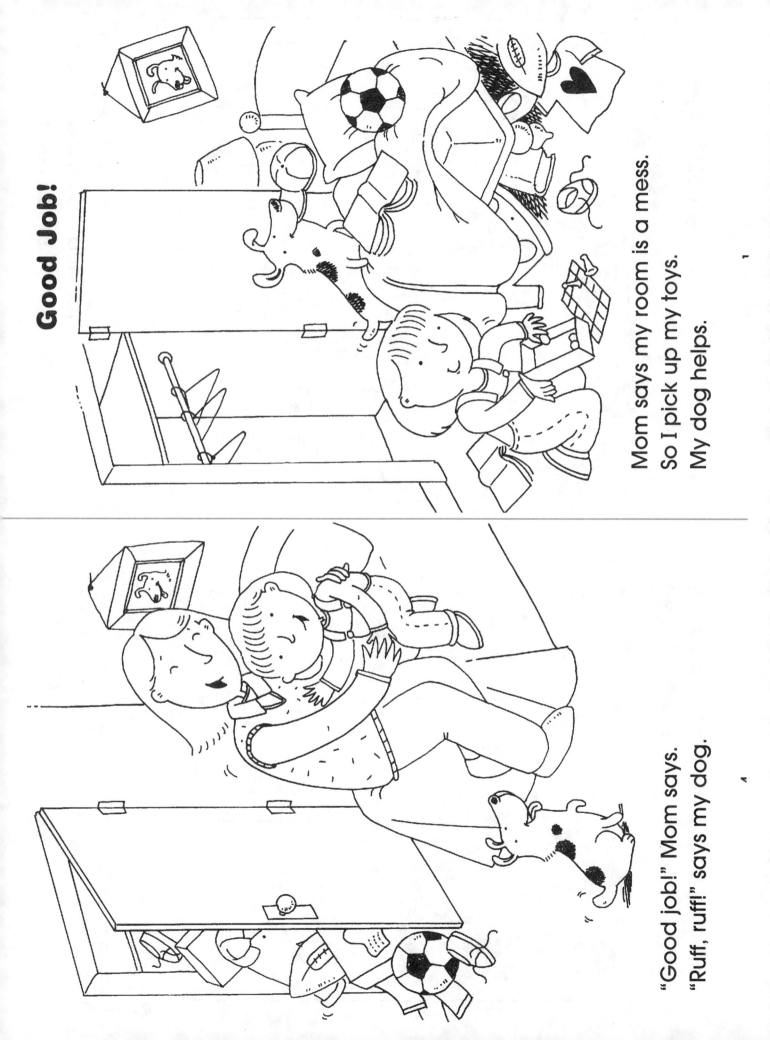

Good Job!

Mom says my room is a mess.
So I pick up my toys.
My dog helps.

1

"Good job!" Mom says.
"Ruff, ruff!" says my dog.

2

I pick up my books.
I pick up my coat and hat.
I make my bed.
My dog helps.

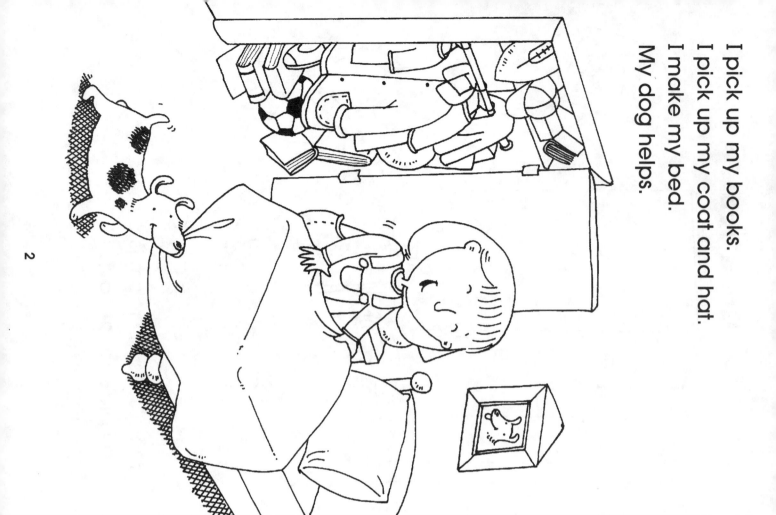

2

Now my room is not a mess.
"How do you like it, Mom?" I ask.

3

Classroom Fun . . .

Beginning and Ending Consonants

Word Walls

Word Walls are a good way to focus on the beginning and ending sounds of letters. For example, if you want to practice the beginning or ending sound of /**p**/, draw a large outline of a panda on butcher paper, cut it out, and post it on the wall. Tell children they may fill the panda with words that begin like *panda* or end like *nap*. Write *panda* at the top of one column, and *nap* at the top of another. During the following days, children can add other words that begin and end with the sound of /**p**/.

Picture Cards

Picture cards can help children practice auditory recognition of beginning and ending sounds and letters. A set of Word/Picture Cards on pages 154–155 will get you started. You can use these cards in the following ways:

• Display several picture cards that illustrate each of three different sounds. Then have students sort the cards according to beginning sounds. Children may also sort the cards according to final sounds.

• Display a letter card or write a letter on the chalkboard. Children can identify picture cards whose names have that beginning or ending sound.

• Have children pair picture cards with words that name them by labeling the cards with stick-on notes or by playing a matching game with the word cards.

Classroom Fun

Letter Cards

You may wish to make letter cards to use in the classroom to practice sound/letter correspondence. Here are some ways you can use the letter cards:

- Say words aloud. Have children hold up the letter card when they hear a word that begins (or ends) with that sound.
- Have children find objects in the classroom that begin or end with a particular letter and attach the letter card to that object. For example, a letter card *p* could be attached to a pencil or poster.
- Say a word and have children choose the letter card that stands for the beginning (or ending) sound.

Word Cards

You can make word cards for high frequency words and words that are highly picturable. A set of Word/Picture Cards on pages 154–155 will get you started. To help children connect sounds to letters, you may wish to use word cards in these ways:

- Children can sort the cards according to beginning and ending sounds.
- Children can match the word cards with picture cards or pictures cut from magazines to identify beginning and ending sounds.
- Partners can play a variation of "Old Maid," dividing the word cards between them and then asking each other if they have a word with a particular beginning or ending sound.

Consonant Scavenger Hunt

Assign a group of children one consonant letter. Give them a time period and let them search the classroom, playground, or other available area for objects whose names begin or end with that consonant. Have children collect the items or draw pictures of the items they find. At the end of the time period, gather the groups together and let them share what they have found.

Pictionary

Children will enjoy making pictionaries. Assign each individual a consonant and have him or her find pictures in magazines or catalogues that begin or end with that sound. Children can cut out the pictures and paste them to a page of construction paper. Bind together all the pages to create a class Consonant Pictionary.

Consonant Bingo

Use the Bingo card pattern on page 153 to play Consonant Bingo with children. Reproduce the page for each player. Tell children to fill in each square with a different consonant letter. (Because there are 24 spaces, they will have to repeat four letters twice.) Give each child markers for the squares, such as small pieces of construction paper. Use the Word Bank on page 156 to call out words. Have children mark the letter square that stands for the beginning consonant sound of that word. When a child has five markers that go across, down, or diagonally, he or she can call out "Bingo!" You may reuse the Bingo card to play again or to practice other skills, such as ending consonant sounds.

What Am I?

Write picturable words on slips of paper. Invite children to take turns drawing a word, writing the beginning or ending consonant on a piece of chart paper, and then drawing a picture that gives a hint about the word's identity. Have classmates guess the word and write it next to the picture.

Missing Letter Riddles

Draw pictures or provide picture cards for words. Write the word for the picture but leave out the beginning or ending consonants. Then have children fill in the missing letters and read the words. You can complete this activity for words of all lengths and difficulty, as long as the words have easily identifiable pictures. See the Word Bank on page 156 for suggested words.

Touchy Feely Letters

Invite children to make "touchy feely" letters by using yarn, beans, seeds, or other tactile objects. Have children use paste to outline the letter, then attach the objects to the paste. Have children trace the letters with their fingers and give examples of objects that begin or end with that letter.

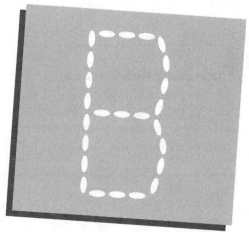

Instant Activities

Consonant Meals Ask children to make up a dinner menu in which the names of all the foods feature a certain consonant sound. For example, a *b* dinner could include broccoli, bagels, beans, and burritos.

Consonant Collage Assign a group a beginning or ending consonant sound. Have children look through magazines to find pictures whose names begin or end with that consonant. Have children cut out the pictures and paste them down to create a collage.

I Spy Play a variation on the game "I Spy." Have children give clues such as "I spy something that ends like *mail.*" *(pail)*

Animal Riddles Partners can create riddles with beginning or ending consonant letters. For example: I'm an animal that flies. I begin with the letter *p*. What am I? *(pigeon)*

Letter of the Day Choose a letter to be the "Letter of the Day." Children can collect objects whose names begin or end with that consonant and place them on a table. At the end of the day, have children identify each object in the collection.

Go Fishing Make a fishing pole with a magnet on the end. Put consonant letter cards attached to paper clips in a plastic pail. Have children fish for a letter and name a word that begins or ends with that sound.

Sandy Letters Give each child a paper plate with a layer of sand or powdered gelatin. As you say a word, have children use their fingers to write in the sand the beginning or ending consonant they hear.

Consonant Bingo Pattern

		Free		

Word Cards

bed	rope	gate	duck
ten	key	pan	nail
leaf	fish	mouse	seal
queen	jeep	hat	web

Picture Cards

Word Bank

Below is a list of words that you may use to illustrate beginning and ending consonant sounds. Some of these words are included in the Word/Picture Card set on pages 154–155. Ideas for using these cards and additional cards you may create yourself can be found in "Classroom Fun," pages 149–151.

——— Beginning Consonants ———

Bb	Hh	Nn	Tt
banana	hat	nail	table
bed	helicopter	nest	ten
box	hill	nine	tiger
Cc	**Jj**	**Pp**	**Vv**
cat	jacket	pan	van
comb	jar	park	vase
cookie	jump rope	pumpkin	violin
Dd	**Kk**	**Qq**	**Ww**
dinosaur	kangaroo	quarter	wagon
dog	key	quilt	water
duck	king	queen	wig
Ff	**Ll**	**Rr**	**Yy**
farm	lamb	ring	yarn
fence	leaf	rope	yellow
foot	lion	rose	yo-yo
Gg	**Mm**	**Ss**	**Zz**
gate	man	seal	zebra
girl	mitten	seven	zipper
goat	mouse	soccer	zoo

——— Ending Consonants ———

b	l	s
bib	ball	bus
cab	bell	dress
tub	hill	gas
d	**m**	**t**
bed	gym	bat
mud	ham	goat
sled	jam	net
f	**n**	**v**
leaf	pan	cave
roof	rain	five
shelf	ten	hive
g	**p**	**x**
flag	cap	box
pig	jeep	fox
rug	map	six
k	**r**	
cake	car	
rake	deer	
truck	jar	

Teacher Notes

Page 132 See page 130, "Working with the Poem."

Page 133 *Answers:* ball, bus; mouse, moon; ten, turtle.

Page 134 *Answers:* farmer, fox, fence; gate, goat, girl; jeep, jacket, jump rope.

Page 135 *Answers:* desk—dog, dinosaur, doll, duck; pumpkin—pillow, potatoes, pie, pot, pencil, puzzle.

Page 136 *Game Directions:* Duplicate the game page and distribute to pairs of children. Say each picture name on the gameboard with children. Then have children cut out the letter cards at the side of the page and place them in a pile face down. They can take turns choosing a letter and advancing a marker to the next picture whose name begins with that sound. Continue until the cub gets home to its mother.

Page 137 *Answers:* red—hydrant, hat, hotel, helicopter, hammer, helmet; blue—wall, window, wagon, woman, water; circles—vase, violin, vest.

Page 138 *Answers:* green—key, king, kitten; yellow—nail, nine, nest.

Page 139 *Answers:* Quinn—quilt, quarter; Yolanda—yarn, yo-yo; Zoe—zebra, zipper.

Page 140 *Answers:* h—hippo, k—kangaroo, p—panda, z—zebra.

Page 141 *Answers:* Matt—hat, goat; Ann—sun, ten; Peg—pig, flag.

Page 142 *Game Directions:* Duplicate the gameboard and distribute to pairs of children. Give each child a marker. Have children cut apart the numbers and place them face down. Each child takes turns choosing a number and moving that number of spaces. The child must say a word that has the same ending sound (*m, b,* or *f*) as the name of the picture in that space. The game continues until one child reaches the finish line.

Page 143 *Answers:* six, car, deer, hive, mailbox, jar, star, box, five, fox.

Page 144 *Answers:* orange—mouse, dress; purple—ball, bell, shell; green—map, rope, lamp.

Page 145 *Answers:* d—bed, sled, cloud, bread, road, bird, braid; k—rock, book, milk, lock, rake, cake, bike, duck, clock.

Page 146 *Answers:* 1. pot, pumpkin; 2. nest, nine; 3. queen, quarter; 4. duck, dog; 5. fox, farmer; 6. flag, pig; 7. bike, cake; 8. bus, dress; 9. hat, goat; 10. ball, bell.

Short & Long Vowels

Using This Book

Classroom Management

Reproducibles Reproducible pages 161–173 offer a variety of individual and partner activities. Simple directions to the children are augmented when necessary by *Answers* or *Game Directions* in the *Teacher Notes* section on page 184.

Directions You may wish to go over the directions with children and verify that they can identify all picture cues before they begin independent work.

Games When children play partner games, you may want to circulate to make sure children understand procedures.

Working with the Poem

A poem on page 160 introduces the phonics elements in this book, short and long vowels. Read this page aloud. Duplicate the poem so that children can work with it in a variety of ways:

Personal Response Read the poem, encouraging children to chime in with you. Then ask children to talk about pets they have.

Phonemic Awareness You can use the poem to introduce or reinforce each vowel sound. Reread the poem and ask children to raise their hands when they hear a particular sound.

Short and Long Vowels Write the poem on a chart and reread the poem with children. Then have children point to or circle words that have the *consonant-vowel-consonant* pattern for short vowel sounds and the *consonant-vowel-consonant-e* pattern for long vowel sounds. Ask children to find one word that has both patterns.

Innovation Brainstorm ideas first. Then duplicate one line or more of the poem, leaving a blank. Encourage children to "write" an original verse.

Connecting School and Home

The Family Letter on page 159 can be sent home to encourage families to reinforce what children are learning. Children will also enjoy sharing the Take-Home Book on pages 175–176. You can cut and fold these booklets ahead of time, or invite children to participate in the process.

Word/Picture Card Sets

Pages 182–183 of this book contain matching sets of Word and Picture Cards drawn from the vocabulary presented in this book. You may wish to mount these on heavier stock as a classroom resource. You may also wish to duplicate and distribute them to children for use in matching and sorting activities. Each child can use a large envelope to store the cards.

Assessment

Page 174, Show What You Know, provides children with targeted practice in standardized test-taking skills, using the content presented in this book.

Dear Family,

Your child is learning in school about words with short and long vowels.

cat   **sun**   **cake**   **mice**

You may enjoy sharing some or all of the following activities with your child:

Use Environmental Print

As you travel around town on foot or in the car, point to signs and environmental print. Ask your child to name any vowel sounds in the words.

Long Vowel Collage

Spend time with your child cutting out pictures of words with long vowel sounds, such as *cake* or *rose*. Paste them on construction paper. Help your child label each picture.

Reading Together

To practice reading words with long and short vowels, read your child's Take-Home Book, "Have You Ever?" Ask your child to color pictures of short vowel words and to circle pictures of long vowel words. You may also wish to look for these books in your local library:

Sincerely,

The Great Big Book of Fun Phonics Activities © Scholastic Professional Books

Name _____

My Pets

My duck ate my cake,
My dog ate my ham,
My cat stole my milk,
And my bee is on my jam.
My pig has my pancake,
My mice got my cheese.
Tell me, why, oh why,
Did I choose pets like these?

Short & Long Vowels

Name _____

Map It Out!

Nan is going to camp. Nan's mom has a map. Help Nan and her mom find the van. Follow the pictures of short **a** words. Draw a line to the van for Nan!

Name _____

Hop, Frog!

Frog wants to hop across the pond to see his friend, Beaver. Write **o** under each picture whose name has the short **o** sound. Draw one more thing Frog can hop on, and write **o** under it on the line. Then cut out Frog and help him hop across the pond.

Name _____

Find a Word

Color all the short **i** words red. Then finish the sentence with the short **i** word you find!

bike	red	hen	time

jam
will
win
with
dog
can
kite
it
pig
lip
lamp
pet
pin
pill
tag
hit
is
fin
hip
ham
wig
hide
get
line
time
hat

Meet me on top of the _____!

Short Vowel Dominoes

Cut out the pictures below. Then play dominoes by matching the pictures whose names have the same vowel sounds. Make new short vowel dominoes by cutting out pictures from magazines.

Rhyming Puzzles

Say the picture names. Cut out the puzzle piece on the right that rhymes with the name of each picture on the left. Paste the puzzle piece where it belongs. Finish the sentence at the bottom of the page.

1.

2.

3.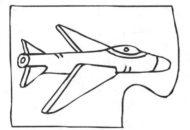

4.

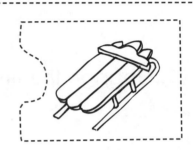

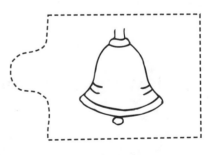

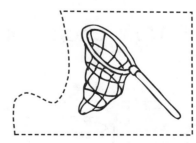

The b _____ ll is on the w _____ ll.

Name _____

Word Ladder

Follow the directions to make new words. Write each new word on the word ladder. Cut and paste the matching picture next to each word.

pup

1. Change the first **p** to **c**.

2. Now, change the **p** to **b**.

3. Now, change the **b** to **t**.

4. Now, change the **c** to **n**.

5. Now, change the **n** to **h**.

Add a Vowel

Look at the consonants next to each number. Add the vowel you hear in the picture to the middle space. Now you have made two words. Read one word from top to bottom. Read the other word from left to right. Write the two words on the lines. Make one word puzzle of your own.

1.

```
      f
  s       n
      n
```

_____

_____

2.

```
          v
  f           n
          n
```

_____

_____

3.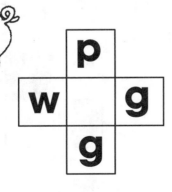

```
      p
  w       g
      g
```

_____

_____

4.

```
      
          
      
```

_____

_____

Crossword Puzzle

Look at each picture clue. Write the picture name in the puzzle next to the matching number. Choose words from the box.

game	rake	tape	vase	cake

Across

2.

4.

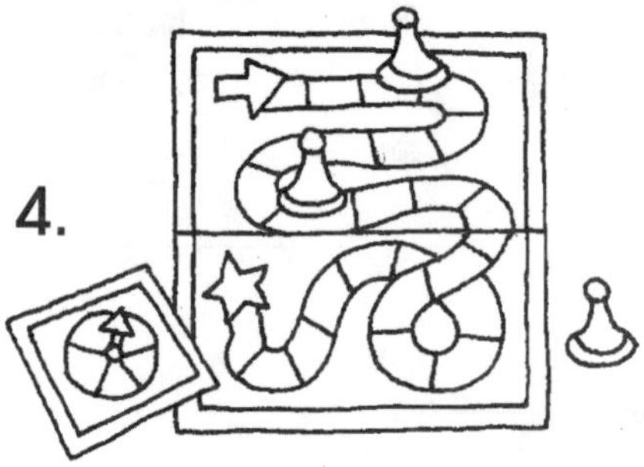

5.

Down

1.

3.

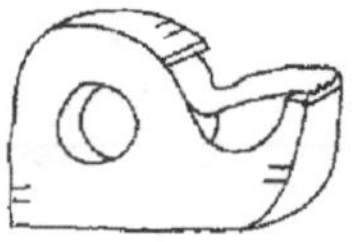

Crossword grid:

1. v
2. a
3. s
4.
   e
5.

Name _____

Riddle Me!

Look at the picture. Read the riddles. Fill in the blank with one of the words in the box.

mice	bike	five	kite	hike

It rides the wind,
It has a white stripe.
It makes me smile.
What is it?
It's my _____.

It can go fast.
It can go slow.
I can ride it by myself.
What is it?
It is a _____.

We walk and we talk,
We look at the birds.
We smell the clean air.
What do we do?
We _____.

Circus Time

Put some long **o** words in the circus! Cut out the long **o** words. Then paste each word in the scene next to the picture it names. Then complete the sentence.

| rope |
| note |
| rose |
| nose |

I need my _____ to smell the _____ !

Long Vowel **o**-consonant-**e**

Name _____

Sliding Words

Cut out the word box and the letter strips. Cut the slits in the word box. Slide letter strips **1** and **2** up and down to make words. Write the words you make.

_____

_____

_____

_____

_____

_____

①	②
t	n
r	t
fl	l
m	b
c	

①	②
u	e

Name _____

A Dog and His Bone

Help the dog find his bone. Your teacher will tell you how to play this game.

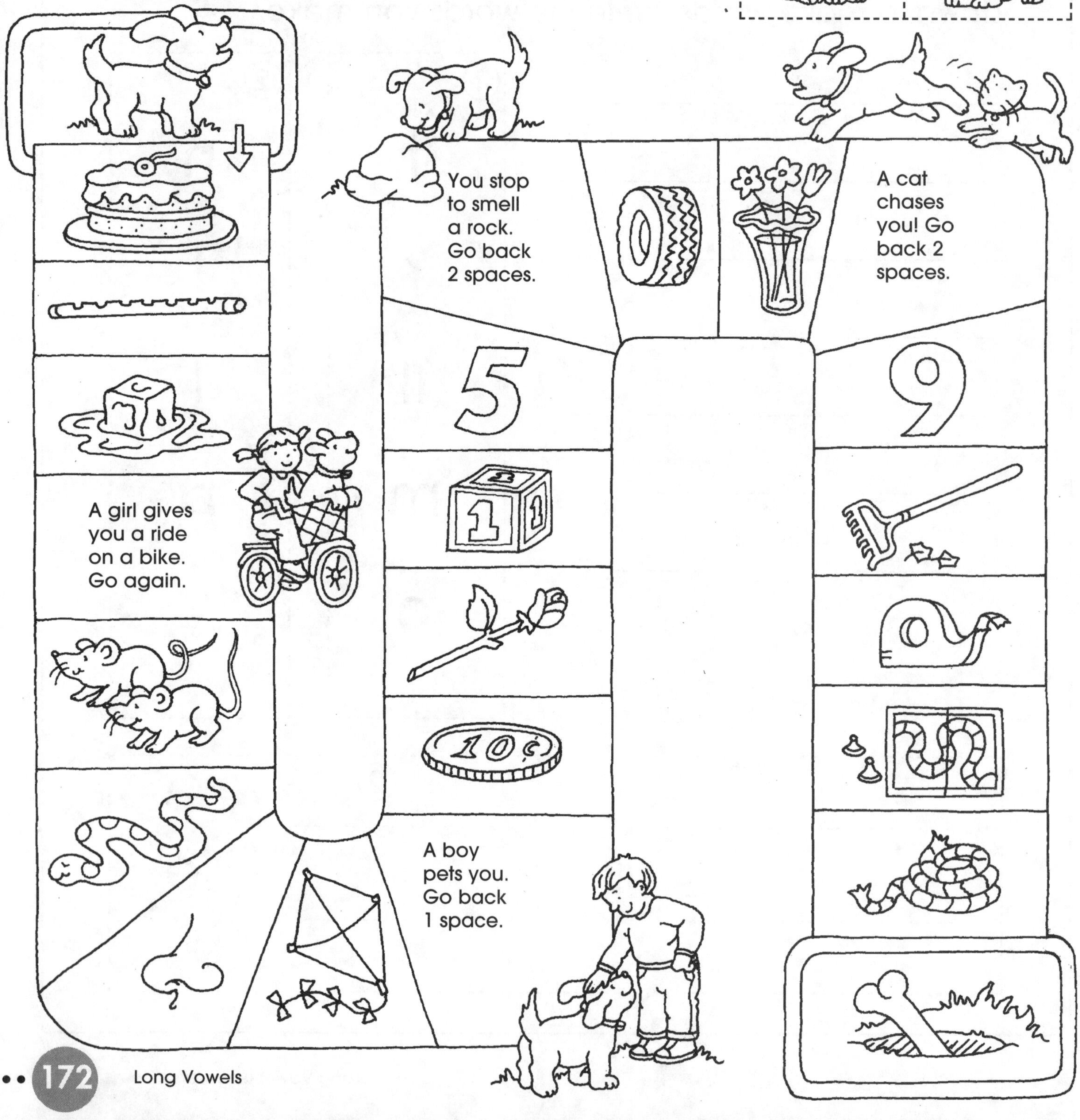

You stop to smell a rock. Go back 2 spaces.

A cat chases you! Go back 2 spaces.

5

9

A girl gives you a ride on a bike. Go again.

A boy pets you. Go back 1 space.

Long Vowels

Name _____

Short and Long Pets

Ann wants pets with short vowel names. Jake wants pets with long vowel names. Write the missing letters to name the pets. Cut out the animal pictures. Paste each one in Jake's box or Ann's box. Color the pictures.

Ann's Pets   **Jake's Pets**

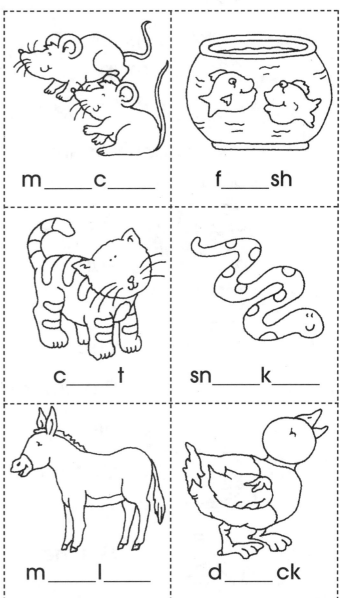

m____c____   f____sh

c____t   sn____k____

m____l____   d____ck

Name _____

Show What You Know

A. Practice taking tests. Look at the pictures. Read the words.
Fill in the circle next to the word that names each picture.

1. ○ fan
   ○ fin
   ○ fine

2. ○ peg
   ○ page
   ○ pig

3. ○ rack
   ○ rake
   ○ ran

4. ○ mope
   ○ map
   ○ mop

5. ○ rise
   ○ rode
   ○ rose

6. ○ well
   ○ will
   ○ web

B. Look at each picture. Say the picture name. Circle the
word that names the picture.

1. The man has a _____.

   van   vine   vest

2. I see the _____.

   cube   pup   cup

3. We can go up the _____.

   hit   hill   hen

4. Can you make a _____?

   rake   lake   cake

5. Get the _____, Lil.

   rope   rose   nose

Have You Ever?

Have you ever seen mice on a hike?

Have you ever seen mice on a hike?

NO!

Have you ever seen
a cub in a bus?

Have you ever seen
a frog with a job?

2

Have you ever seen
a hen in a jet?

Have you ever seen
a mule sing a tune?

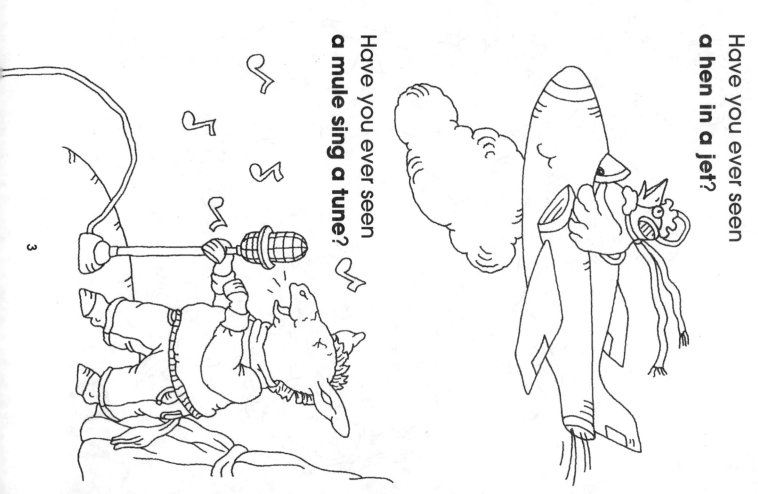

3

Classroom Fun ...

Vowel Zoo

Invite children to brainstorm a list of zoo animals whose names have long and short vowel sounds. (For example: *crocodile, hippo, elephant, ostrich, snake, ape,* and so on.) Provide magazines and drawing materials so children can cut out or create pictures of the animals. Have them paste each picture onto oaktag, bending back 3 or 4 inches at the bottom to create a stand-up frame. A length or two of tape in the back will help the frame stand up more securely. Have children make a label for each animal. Place the frames in an alphabet zoo, arranging each animal in a display according to the vowel sound in its name.

Letter Cards

You may wish to distribute letter cards for vowels and consonants in order to practice sound/letter correspondence. Here are some ways you can use them:

- Say words aloud. Have children hold up the vowel card that matches the vowel sound in each word.
- Call out a word, such as *can* or *cane*, and have children arrange the letter cards to make the word.
- Write short vowel words such as *can, tub,* or *cub* on the chalkboard. Have children recreate each word with letter cards. Then have children add the letter card *e* to each word and read the new word they have made.

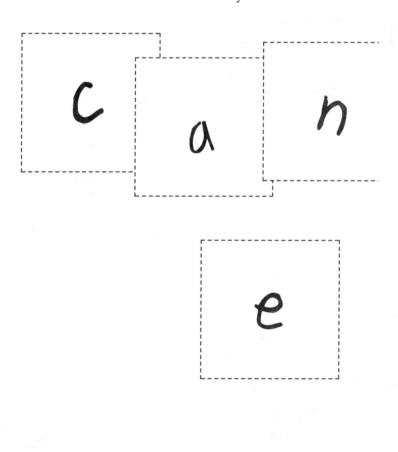

Classroom Fun

Picture Cards

Picture cards can help children practice auditory recognition of long and short vowels. A set of Word/Picture Cards on pages 182–183 will get you started. You can use these cards in the following ways:

- Display several picture cards for each of three different vowel sounds. Then have children sort the cards according to vowel sounds.
- Display a vowel letter card or write a vowel on the chalkboard. Have children identify picture cards whose names have that vowel sound.
- Have children match picture cards with word cards or label the picture cards with stick-on notes.

Spin a Vowel Sound Game

Make spinners from the pattern on page 181 by cutting each circle and the arrow shape out of oaktag. Push a paper fastener though the arrow in the center of the spinner. Press the fastener tails down flat. Before you use each spinner, say each picture name and identify the vowel sound. Have children form teams and take turns spinning the spinner, landing on a picture, and naming another word with that same vowel sound. A team gets a point for each word a child can correctly name.

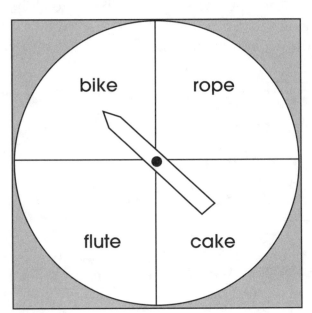

Word Ladders

On the chalkboard, begin a word ladder by writing *cat*. Ask children how they might change the beginning consonant *c* in order to make a new word. For example, they might change the *c* to *h* to make the word *hat*. Show children how to change the ending consonant, and finally suggest changing the vowel. To reinforce the long vowel sounds, start a new ladder with the vowel-consonant-*e* pattern.

cat	lake
hat	cake
ham	wake
him	woke
hit	poke
hot	pole
cot	hole
lot	home

"Vowel Says" Game

Play a version of "Simon Says." Instead of beginning with "Simon says," tell children to follow your instructions only when they hear a person's name that has a short vowel sound. For example:

Kim says, "Close your eyes." *(yes)*
Ben says, "Stand up." *(yes)*
Pam says, "Sit down." *(yes)*
Pat says, "Touch your toes." *(yes)*
Joe says, "Put on your coat." *(no)*
Luke says, "Raise your hands up." *(no)*
Jill says, "Touch your chin." *(yes)*
Jane says, "Go outside." *(no)*

You may want to play this game again using names with long vowel sounds.

Short or Long Charades

Place short and long vowel word cards in a bag or box. Divide the class into teams. To begin the game, have a volunteer reach in to the bag to choose a word card. The child can gesture to indicate whether the word has a long or short sound. Then have the child act out the word and let children on the other team guess what it is. Easy Words: *cat, pig, ax, race, rake, frog, snake, jump.* Harder Words: *flag, camp, mud, shop, cake, rope, rose, kite.*

Short or Long Vowel Mobiles

Cut out a large picture shape of a word representing a vowel sound (such as *cat* for short *a*, *bell* for short *e*, *pig* for short *i*, *top* for short *o*, and *bus* for short *u*). Then give a small group of children one of the shapes. Ask them to think of other examples of objects whose names have that vowel sound. Let them color and cut out pictures of each object and attach them to the large shape with yarn. Each group can present its mobile to the class.

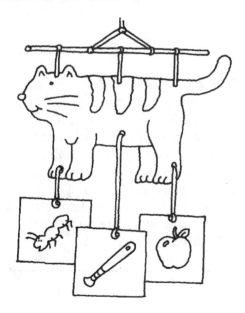

Instant Activities

Rhyme It Say a short or long vowel word, and have children say a word that rhymes. Continue, until the list is exhausted. Then let another child say a long or short vowel word, and continue.

Listen and Walk Ask children to stand in a straight line facing you, but ten steps away. As you say two words, have them take a step forward if the two words have the same vowel sound. Use pairs like these: *lake, game; ice, pig; cab, trash.*

Vowel Concentration Write words on index cards, two for each long and short vowel sound. Turn them face down and have children take turns turning over two, trying to make a vowel sound match. If the two vowel sounds do match, the player keeps the cards. If not, the cards are turned back over. Play until all cards have been matched.

Silly Sentences Have children choose a short or long vowel sound. Then, have them use two or more words with that vowel sound in a silly sentence. For example: *My black cat goes to camp.*

Secret Sentences Write sentences with missing short vowels and have children try to figure out what the sentence says. For example: *The p_g h_s on a b_g r_d w_g.* Then challenge children to create secret sentences of their own.

Tic-Tac-Toe Children can play tic-tac-toe with short vowel words instead of X's and O's. Draw a tic-tac-toe grid on the chalkboard. Have two children come to the chalkboard and take turns wrting a word with a certain short vowel sound. The first one to be able to draw a line through three items in a row with the same vowel sound wins the game.

Bag of Vowels Place word cards for short or long vowels on a desk next to bags labeled for each category. Have children take turns reading a word and placing the card in the appropriate bag.

Spin-a-Vowel-Sound Pattern

Spinner 1: Long Vowels

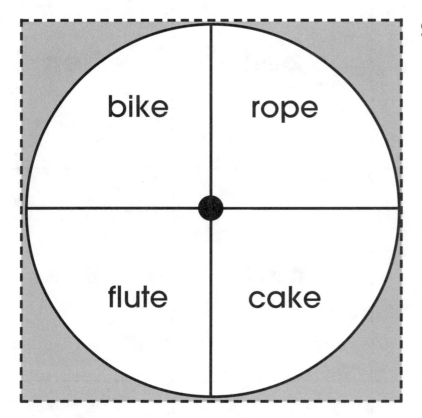

bike | rope

flute | cake

Spinner 2: Short Vowels

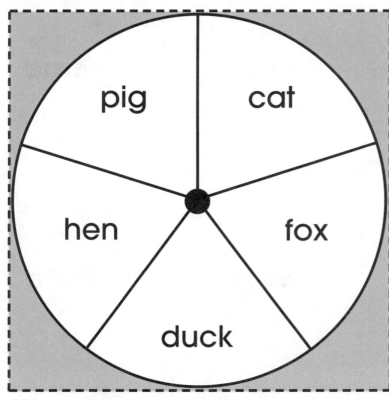

pig | cat

hen | fox

duck

Word Cards

cat	fan	bell	hen
pig	hill	mop	bus
sun	game	lake	dime
bike	rose	note	flute

Picture Cards

Word Bank

Below is a list of words that you may use to illustrate short and long vowel sounds. Some of these words are included in the Word/Picture Card set on pages 182–183. Ideas for using these cards and additional cards you may create yourself can be found in "Classroom Fun," pages 177–179.

──── **Short Vowels** ────

a
ax
bag
bat
cat
cap
fan
fat
ham
hat
jam
map
pan
tag
van

e
bed
bell
egg
hen
jet
pen
pet

red
ten
web
well

i
bib
fig
hill
lid
lip
pig
pin
six
wig
win
win

o
cot
fog
hot
jog
lock

log
mop
pop
top

u
bus
club
cub
cup
cut
fun
hut
mud
nut
pup
sub
sun

──── **Long Vowels** ────

a
ape
cage
cake
cape
cane
cave
game
lake
name
race
rake
tape
vase

i
bike
dime
dive
five
hike
ice
kite
line

mice
nine
rice
ride
time
vine

o
bone
hole
home
joke
mole
nose
note
robe
rope
rose
woke

u
cube
cute
flute
mule
rude
rule
tube
tune
use

Teacher Notes

Page 160 See page 158, "Working with the Poem."

Page 161 *Answers:* trash cans, caps, flags, cat, cab, man, fan, bags, van; Bonus Words: map, sunglasses.

Page 162 *Answers:* rock, box, dog.

Page 163 *Answers:* with, lip, pill, hip, hit, it, is, will, pig, fin, win, pin, wig; hill.

Page 164 *Answers:* short vowel *a*-flag, map, lamp, van, fan, cat, hat, bat; short vowel *i*- pig, wig, fish, six, bib, hill; short vowel *o*- sock, clock, log, mop, dog, rock.

Page 165 *Answers:* 1. well-bell 2. hen-ten 3. jet-net 4. bed-sled   The bell is on the well.

Page 166 *Answers:* 1. cup 2. cub 3. cut 4. nut 5. hut.

Page 167 *Answers:* 1. fun, sun; 2. van, fan; 3. pig, wig; 4. Answers will vary.

Page 168 *Answers:* 1. vase 2. cake 3. tape 4. game 5. rake.

Page 169 *Answers:* kite, bike, hike.

Page 170 *Answers:* nose, rose, rope, note; I need my nose to smell the rose!

Page 171 *Answers:* tune, tube, rule, flute, mute, mule, cute, cube.

Page 172 Game Directions: Distribute gameboards to pairs of children. Tell them to cut out the dog pictures to use as markers. Before playing, say all the picture names with children. Then have the first player toss a number cube and move that number of spaces. To stay on a picture space a child must say the picture name and the name of the vowel sound. It is then the next player's turn, unless the space has special instructions. Play continues until the dog reaches his bone.

Page 173 *Answers:* Ann: cat, fish, duck; Jake: mice, mule, snake.

Page 174 *Answers:* A. 1. fan 2. pig 3. rake 4. mop 5. rose 6. web; B. 1. van 2. cup 3. hill 4. cake 5. rope.

Consonant Blends & Digraphs

Using This Book

Classroom Management

Reproducibles Reproducible pages 189–201 offer a variety of individual and partner activities. Simple directions to the children are augmented when necessary by *Answers* or *Game Directions* in the *Teacher Notes* Section on page 212.

Directions You may wish to go over the directions with children and verify that they can identify all picture cues before they begin independent work.

Games When children play partner games, you may want to circulate in order to make sure that children understand procedures.

Working with the Poem

A poem on page 188 introduces the phonics elements in this book, consonant blends and digraphs. Start by reading this page aloud to children. Duplicate the poem so that children can work with it in a variety of ways:

Personal Response Read the poem aloud and have children talk about it. Ask children if they have a favorite season of the year.

Phonemic Awareness Read the poem aloud each day. Ask children to listen for a particular beginning or ending consonant blend or digraph and to raise their hands when they hear it.

Sound to Letter Write the poem on a chart, and ask children to point to or circle words that begin or end with consonant blends or digraphs.

Innovation Brainstorm ideas first. Duplicate one line of the poem, leaving a blank. Encourage children to "write" an original verse by filling in the blank.

Connecting School and Home

The Family Letter on page 187 can be sent home to encourage families to reinforce what children are learning. Children will also enjoy sharing the Take-Home Book on pages 203–204. You can cut and fold these booklets ahead of time, or invite children to participate in the process. You may also mount the pages on heavier stock so you can place the Take-Home Book in your classroom library.

Word/Picture Card Sets

Pages 210–211 of this book contain matching sets of Word/Picture Cards drawn from the vocabulary presented in this book. You may wish to mount these on heavier stock as a classroom resource. You may also wish to duplicate and distribute them to children for use in matching and sorting activities. Each child can use a large envelope to store the cards.

Assessment

Page 202, Show What You Know, provides children with targeted practice in standardized test-taking skills, using the content presented in this book in the assessment items.

Dear Family,

Your child is learning in school about consonant blends and digraphs.

In a consonant blend, the sound of each consonant letter is heard. Some consonant blends are **pl, sn, st,** and **tr**.

In a consonant digraph, two consonants stand for one sound. Some consonant digraphs are **sh, ch, wh**, and **th**.

tree

ship

You may enjoy sharing some or all of the following activities with your child:

Tongue Twisters

With your child, make a list of words that begin or end with the consonant digraphs **sh, ch, wh,** and **th**. Use some of the words to make a sentence that is a tongue twister. (Example: *Shy Shirley sells seashells*.) See who can say the sentence faster!

Consonant Blend Search

On a car trip with your child, look together for words on signs that begin with consonant blends, such as **br**ick, **gr**een, **tr**ack, **sp**orts, and **st**op. Write down the words. When you get home, read the words. What blend did you find most often?

Reading Together

To practice reading words with consonant blends and digraphs, look through your child's Take-Home Book, "What Time Is It?" Help your child circle words with consonant blends and digraphs. You may also wish to look for the following books in your local library:

Sincerely,

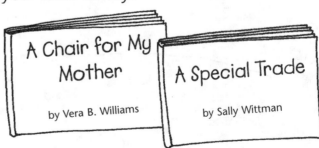

A Chair for My Mother

by Vera B. Williams

A Special Trade

by Sally Wittman

Name _____

Spring

A flower blooms,
A soft wind blows,
Fish splash in the pond,
And green grass grows.
A bird flies north,
While children swing.
Check, watch, and find
Each sign of spring!

Consonant Blends & Digraphs

Name _____

Honey Hunt

Help Big Bear find the honey. Follow pictures on the path whose names **begin** or **end** with **sh**. Draw a path for Big Bear.

What Goes Together?

What goes together? Draw a line to match each picture on the left to a picture on the right. Color the pictures whose names **begin** or **end** with **sh**.

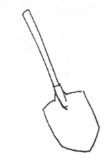

Digraph **sh**

Name _____

Cheese for Lunch

This mouse is hungry — but so is the cat! Look at the picture. Circle seven hidden pictures whose names **begin** with **ch**. Fill in the blanks to find out what the mouse is saying.

Name _____

Hoop Fun

What should these players do?
Color in the spaces with words that **begin**
or **end** with **ch**. Read the word you have
made. Write the word in the sentence at
the bottom of the page.

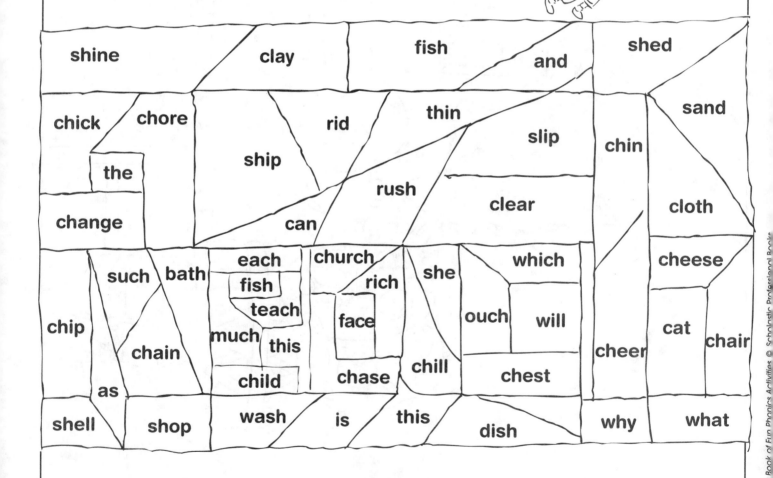

shine	clay	fish / and	shed
chick / chore	rid	thin	sand
the	ship	slip	chin
change	can	rush / clear	cloth
such bath	each / fish / teach	church / rich / she	which	cheese
chip	much / this	face	ouch will	cat / chair
chain	child	chase / chill	chest	cheer
as				
shell	shop	wash is this dish	why	what

_____ up high!

Name _____

Bedtime

Help Lin tell her bedtime story.
Choose a picture to fill each space.
Write **th** to **begin** or **end** the word in each box.

I go to bed at seven [____] .

First I brush my [____] .

It is fun to take a [____] .

I [____] it's time to sleep.

___ ___ irty

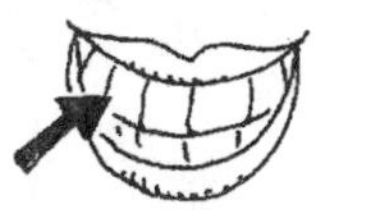

tee ___ ___

ba ___ ___

___ ___ ink

The Great Big Book of Fun Phonics Activities © Scholastic Professional Books

Name _____

What's Going On?

Look at each picture box. Find one thing in the picture whose name **begins** with **wh** and color it. Write the word that names it. Use the words in the box.

whistle	whiskers	wheel	whale

1.

_____

2.

_____

3.

_____

4.

_____

Make a Wish

Look at the pictures one at a time. Write the two letters that **begin** each picture name. Then color a coin in the well that has the same two letters. Use the letters on the last coin to answer the question.

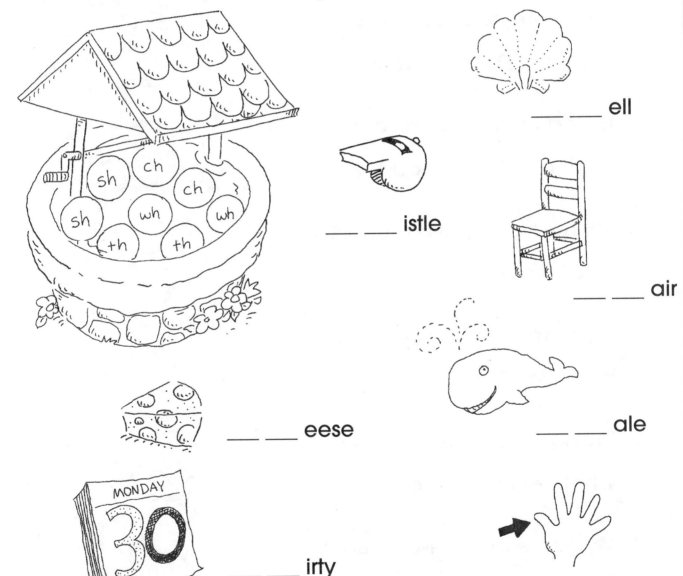

___ ___ ell

___ ___ istle

___ ___ air

___ ___ eese

___ ___ ale

___ ___ irty

___ ___ umb

What did you wish? ____ ____ ! Don't tell.

Name _____

Name _____

What Am I?

Read each clue. Write the two letters that **begin** each word. Then draw a line to the picture that matches the word.

1. My name begins like **gr**een.

   What am I? ___ ___**apes**

2. My name begins like **br**own.

   What am I? ___ ___**ead**

3. My name begins like **cr**ayon.

   What am I? ___ ___**ib**

4. My name begins like **tr**eat.

   What am I? ___ ___**ain**

5. My name begins like **fr**iend.

   What am I? ___ ___**og**

6. My name begins like **dr**eam.

   What am I? ___ ___**ess**

r Blends **br, cr, dr, fr, gr, tr**

Name _____

Get the Dragon!

Play "Get the Dragon" with a classmate. Your teacher will tell you how to play the game.

1
2
1
2
1
2
1
2
1
2

r Blends **br, cr, dr, fr, gr, tr**   197

Match It!

Draw lines to match the pictures that **begin** with the same sounds. Then write the letters that show how the names of each picture pair begin. Choose letter blends from the box.

fl	gl	pl	cl	bl

1.   _____

2.   _____

3.   _____

4.  _____

5.   _____

Name _____

Fly Around the World

Help the plane fly around the world. Your teacher will tell you how to play.

| block   flowers   clock   clown   flute   glass   plug |

4. _____

5. _____

3. _____

6.  _____

2.  _____

7. _____

1.  _____

Airport

Skate or Slide

Play Skate or Slide with a friend. Your teacher will tell you how to play this game.

		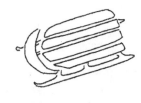

	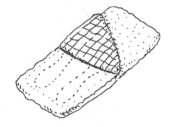	

s Blends **sk, sl**

Name _____

Crossword Puzzle

Look at each picture clue. Read the words in the box.
Write each picture name in the puzzle.

| snake | spider | stop | snail | smoke |

1. s _ _ _ _
   t
   o
2. p _ _ _ _
3. _ _ _ _ _

Across

1.

2.

3.

Down

1.

2.

Name _____

Show What You Know

Read the letters that begin each row. Think of the sound or sounds they stand for. Find the pictures whose names begin with the same two letters. Fill in the circle next to those pictures.

1. sh ○    ○   ○

2. wh ○    ○    ○

3. ch ○   ○    ○

4. br ○   ○    ○

5. cl ○    ○   ○

6. sn ○   ○   ○

7. tr ○   ○   ○

8. sk ○   ○   ○

Standardized Test-Taking Skills

The Great Big Book of Fun Phonics Activities © Scholastic Professional Books

What Time Is It?

Time to get dressed!
Time to put on my socks and sneakers!
Time to eat breakfast!

1

Time to sleep with my black bear!
Time to close my eyes and dream!
Good night!

4

Time for lunch!
Time for yummy chicken!
Time to go back to class!

Time to take the bus home!
Time to slide on my new sled!
Time for fun in the snow!

Classroom Fun .....

Consonant Blends and Digraphs

A Stepping Stone Walk

Cut out twenty "stepping stones" from heavy paper, and write each of these blends on two stones: *br, gr, tr, bl, cl, pl, sp, st, sm, sn.* Lay the stones out on the floor, securing them with masking tape. Divide the class into two teams. Use the Consonant Blend Spinner Pattern on page 209 to spin for blends, or designate a child to be the official Spinner. After the first spin, a player from Team 1 moves to the first stone that has the correct blend and says a word that begins with that blend. If the player can't think of a word, he or she goes to the back of the line. Then Team 2 takes a turn. If two players land on the same stone, the person already there is "bumped" to the back of the line. The first team to get all players to the last stone wins!

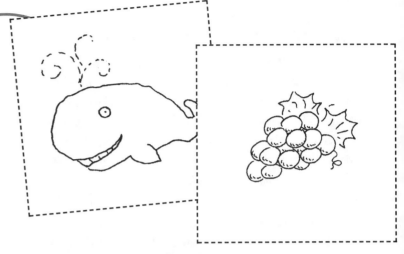

Picture Cards

Have children use the Picture Cards from page 31 or make their own picture cards of words that begin with consonant digraphs and blends. (See the Word Bank on page 212 for suggested words.) Write a blend or digraph on each of several paper bags or boxes, and have children sort the cards according to the different beginning sounds. You may also want to use the Word Cards from page 210 or create your own word cards, and have children match words to pictures.

Blend and Digraph Concentration

Have children use their own picture cards along with those on page 211 to play "Concentration." Make sure there are two cards for each blend or digraph. Shuffle the cards and lay them all face down. Then have pairs of children take turns turning over two cards at a time, looking for pictures whose names have the same beginning sounds. If a child turns over two cards that match, he or she may keep the cards. If not, the cards must be turned face down again and play goes to the other child. When all the cards have been picked up, the player with the most cards wins the game.

Classroom Fun

Classroom Story Time

Choose a consonant blend or digraph, such as *sn* or *ch,* and have children brainstorm a list of words with those beginning (and/or ending) letters. Then have them create a class story with the words. Write a sentence on the board to get children started, such as *Once upon a time, a rich king declared that all cherries must be eaten at the beach. So, ...* Call on volunteers to add a sentence that continues the story and has at least one word with the target blend or digraph. Encourage children to have fun making up a silly story.

Classroom Search for Blends and Digraphs

Have children help you gather objects commonly found in the classroom, such as a clock, chalk, cloth, dish, wheel, crayon, broom, frame, fruit, block, globe, shoes, snapshot, and things that are black, blue, brown, green, gray, or white. Display the objects on a table and have children tell what beginning sound and letters each object's name, material, or color begins with. Then have them sort the objects according to beginning sounds.

Word Walls

Word Walls are a good way to focus on consonant blends and digraphs. For example, if you want to practice the beginning or ending sound of /**sh**/, draw a large outline of a ship on brown wrapping paper, cut it out, and post it on the wall. Tell children they may fill the ship with words that begin like *ship* or end like *dish.* Write *ship* at the top of one column, and *dish* at the top of another. Encourage children to write words or draw pictures of objects with names that begin or end with *sh* in the correct column. Later, read aloud the words with the class and invite volunteers to take turns creating sentences with the words. Use the same idea to practice other blends and digraphs.

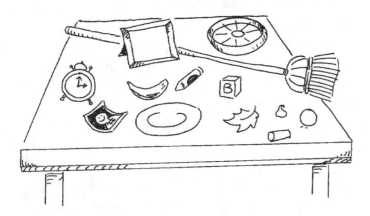

Letter Cards

Help children understand how two consonant letters are blended together. Make separate letter cards for the blends. Then spread out the letters along the chalk rail and help children create words. Begin with these words: *lock, rot, last, lap, top, tar, tick, port, pace, pot, nail, lug,* and *led.* Then have them add one consonant to each word to make these words: *clock, trot, blast, clap, stop, star, stick, sport, space, spot, snail, plug,* and *sled.*

Make a Digraph

Print these words on the chalkboard and have volunteers use a different-colored chalk to add a consonant to each word so that it begins with a digraph: *case (chase); hoot (shoot); hat (chat, that); tin (thin); hop (shop, chop); hip (ship, chip); sell (shell); hen (then, when); tank (thank).* If children are adding the second consonant, they should erase the first one and rewrite both consonants. Have children say the word before and after they make the digraph.

Go-Together Words

Have children brainstorm a list of words for *r, l,* or *s* consonant blends, such as *bread, dress, truck, frog, grapes, train, green; plane, clock, flag, flute, black, blue; skunk, slide, sleep, snake, spider.* Then have them sort the words into categories, such as *color words, food words,* and *transportation words.* Encourage them to come up with their own categories, such as *scary words, animal words,* and *loud words.* You can also divide the class into two teams and have teams take turns suggesting words. Award a point to the team that says the last word with each blend.

Instant Activities

Act It Out Children can take turns acting out different action words that begin or end with a blend or digraph, such as *wash, catch, touch, reach, grin, break, whisper, shop, close, shut, blow, spend, sniff, snuggle, snore,* and *sneeze* while classmates guess the word. You may want to have the actor provide the blend or digraph as a clue.

Name Game Encourage children to think of first names that begin or end with consonant blends or digraphs. List the names on the chalkboard and have children sort them according to their beginning or ending sounds. (Examples: *Shayla, Seth, Brianna, Stacy, Theo, Tish.*)

Digraph Search Invite pairs of children to look through a favorite book and find words (or picture names) that begin or end with a particular consonant digraph. Set a time limit of two minutes. Invite the pairs to dictate the words they have found. Write the words on chart paper.

Beginning or End? Divide the class into two groups. Tell children you will say some words. If a word **begins** with *th, ch,* or *sh,* Group 1 should stand up. If a word **ends** with *th, ch,* or *sh,* Group 2 should stand up. Say these words: *peach, chair, sandwich, shell, fish, thirty, cherry, much, touch, that, beneath, thick, dish, shadow, teeth, cheese*

Hot Potato Blend Game Arrange children in a circle. Pass around a bean bag (the "hot potato") and say a chant such as "Round and round we go — when I stop, say a word that begins like *star.*" The child who is holding the "potato" when you finish saying the chant must say a word with the same beginning consonant blend. Allow plenty of thinking time!

Find a Picture Encourage pairs or small groups of children to hunt quickly through magazines for pictures of items whose names begin or end with *sh, ch, wh,* and *th.* Then have each child paste a picture on a card and write or dictate a sentence that goes with it.

S-Blend Musical Chairs Arrange chairs as if you are playing Musical Chairs. Have children circle around the chairs as you say a list of words. When they hear a word that begins with an *s* blend (such as *story* or *slide*), they must try to find a chair and sit down.

Consonant Blend Spinner Pattern

To make a Consonant Blend Spinner, cut out the circle and paste it to a piece of oaktag or poster board. Cut out the spinner arrow and mount it on oaktag. Push a paper fastener through the center of the arrow and then through the center of the circle. Press the fastener's tails down, make sure the arrow spins freely, and spin the arrow.

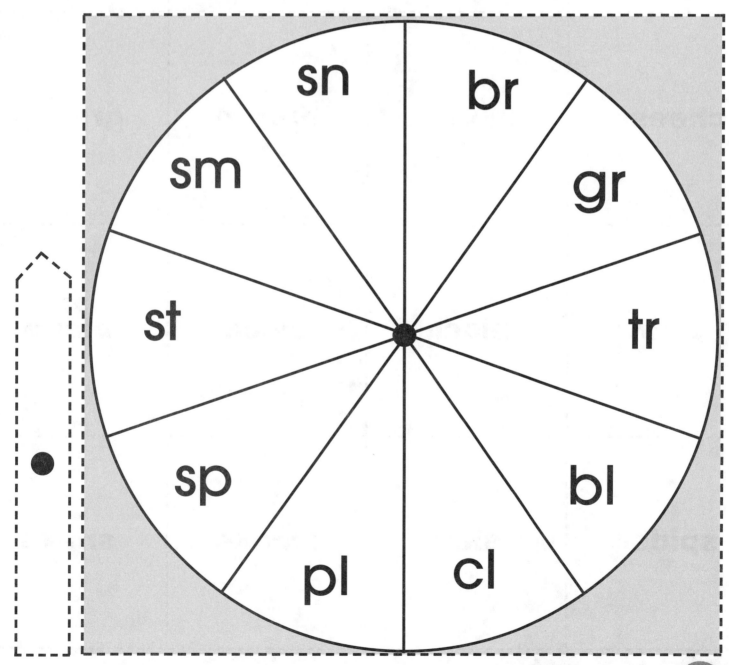

The Great Big Book of Fun Phonics Activities © Scholastic Professional Books

Word Cards

ship	fish	thumb	teeth
cheese	whale	broom	grapes
train	block	clock	plane
spider	sled	smoke	snake

Picture Cards

Word Bank

Below is a list of words that illustrate beginning and ending consonant digraphs and beginning consonant blends. Some of these words are included in the Word/Picture Card set on pages 210–211. Ideas for using these cards can be found in "Classroom Fun," pages 205–207.

Consonant Digraphs (Beginning and Ending)

sh
sheep
shelf
ship
hush
wash
wish

th
thing
think
thumb
cloth
moth
teeth

ch
chase
child
chin
beach
rich
teach

wh
what
wheel
when
where
whisper
why

Consonant Blends (Beginning)

br
broom
brown
brush

cr
crab
crayon
crow

dr
dragon
draw
drive

fr
Friday
friend
fruit

gr
grape
grin
grow

tr
track
trail
truck

bl
black
blow
blue

cl
clay
club
climb

fl
flag
floor
fly

gl
glad
glove
glue

pl
plan
planets
plastic

sk
ski
skirt
skunk

sl
sled
sleeve
slow

sp
space
spin
sports

st
stairs
stamp
stay

sm
small
smell
smile

sn
snake
sneeze
snow

Teacher Notes

Page 188 See page 186, "Working with the Poem."

Page 189 *Answers:* ship, shell, fish, shovel, dish, shoe, shirt, brush.

Page 190 *Preparation:* Ask children to name some things that go together, such as *salt* and *pepper*. Answers: shovel, fish, shoes, brush, dish.

Page 191 *Answers:* chair, chimney, cherries, church, chest, chick, cheese; **ch**eese.

Page 192 *Answers:* chick, chore, change, chip, such, chain, each, teach, much, child, church, rich, chase, chill, which, ouch, chest, chin, cheer, cheese, chair; Reach.

Page 193 *Answers:* 1. thirty 2. teeth 3. bath 4. think.

Page 194 *Answers:* 1. wheel 2. whiskers 3. whale 4. whistle.

Page 195 *Answers:* sh—shell; ch—cheese, chair; th—thumb, thirty; wh—whale, whistle; Sh!

Page 196 *Answers:* 1. grapes 2. bread 3. crib 4. train 5. frog 6. dress.

Page 197 *Game Directions:* Arrange children in pairs. Players take turns choosing a number card and moving that number of spaces. The player says the word in the space and then says another word that begins with the same blend. If a child cannot think of a word, he or she must move back to the previous space. The first player to reach the dragon wins.

Page 198 *Answers:* flowers, flute, **fl**; glove, glass, **gl**; plane, planets, **pl**; block, blanket, **bl**; cloud, clock, **cl**.

Page 199 *Game Directions:* Have children color and cut out the airplane game marker, and tell children to place the plane marker on the runway at the Airport. At each stop the player must say the picture name, write the name (using words from the box), and then color the picture. Tell children to continue around the world until they return to the Airport. *Answers:* 1. flowers 2. block 3. clown 4. clock 5. plug 6. flute 7. glass.

Page 200 *Game Directions:* Have children play in pairs. Have them cut out the pictures, mix them up, and place them in a pile face down. The first player calls out either "skate" or "slide." He or she then chooses a picture card and says the name out loud. If it begins with the same sound as the word that was called out, the player keeps the card. If not, the player must return the card to the bottom of the pile. A smiley face card is "free" and may be used to match either "skate" or "slide." The winner is the player with the most cards at the end.

Page 201 *Answers:* Across: 1. smoke 2. spider 3. snail; Down: 1. stop 2. snake.

Page 202 *Answers:* 1. ship, shell 2. whale, wheel, 3. cheese, chair 4. bread, broom, 5. clock, clown 6. snail, snake 7. triangle, tree 8. skirt, skunk.

Vowel Digraphs

Using This Book

Classroom Management

Reproducibles Reproducible pages 217–229 offer a variety of individual and partner activities. Simple directions to the children are augmented when necessary by *Answers or Game Directions* in the *Teacher Notes* section on page 240.

Directions You may wish to go over the directions with children and verify that they can identify all picture cues and read any words in the activities before they begin independent work.

Games When children play partner games, you may want to circulate in order to make sure children understand procedures.

Working with the Poem

A poem on page 216 introduces the phonics element in this book, vowel digraphs. Read this page aloud to children. Duplicate the poem so that children can work with it in a variety of ways:

Personal Response Read the poem aloud and have children talk about it.

Phonemic Awareness Have children listen for a particular vowel sound as you read the poem aloud.

Sound to Letter Write the poem on chart paper, and have children circle words with vowel digraphs.

Dramatization Encourage groups of three children to perform the poem, with one taking the role of the sun, one taking the role of the moon, and one reading the narration in between.

Connecting School and Home

The Family Letter on page 215 can be sent home to encourage families to reinforce what children are learning. Children will also enjoy sharing the Take-Home Book on pages 231–232. You can cut and fold these booklets ahead of time, or invite children to participate in the process. You may also mount the pages on heavier stock and place the Take-Home Book in your classroom library.

Word/Picture Card Sets

Pages 238–239 of this book contain matching sets of Word/Picture Cards drawn from the vocabulary presented in this book. You may wish to mount these on heavier stock as a classroom resource. You may also wish to duplicate and distribute them to children for use in matching and sorting activities. Each child can use a large envelope to store the cards.

Assessment

Page 230, Show What You Know, provides children with targeted practice in standardized test-taking skills, using the content presented in this book in the assessment items.

Dear Family,

Your child is learning in school about vowel digraphs.

In a vowel digraph, two vowel letters together stand for one vowel sound. Some vowel digraphs are **ai, ea, oo, ie,** and **oa**.

train

boat

tie

You may enjoy sharing some or all of the following activities with your child:

Rhyme a Word

Ask your child to play a rhyming game. Say a word such as *mail, day, bean, feed, tie, goat,* or *book* and ask children to say as many rhyming words as he or she can think of.

Comic Book Search

Use the comics section of the newspaper or a comic book to look for words with these vowel pairs: *ai, ay, ea, ee,* and *oa.* Circle each word. Then read the comics together.

Reading Together

To practice reading words with vowel digraphs, look through your child's Take-Home Book, "A Book of Riddles." Ask your child to underline words with vowel digraphs and to read the words for you.

You may also wish to look for these books in your local library:

Sincerely,

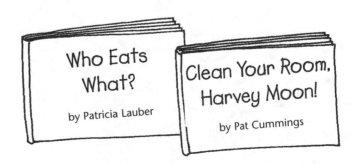

Who Eats What?
by Patricia Lauber

Clean Your Room, Harvey Moon!
by Pat Cummings

Name _____

Good Afternoon

"Good afternoon,"
Said the sun to the moon.
"I feel weak and could use a break."
Said the moon with a yawn,
"I can stay until dawn.
You sleep, and I'll keep awake!"

Vowel Digraphs

The Great Big Book of Fun Phonics Activities © Scholastic Professional Books

Name _____

Gently Down the Stream

Follow Jean down the stream. Color all the pictures whose long **e** names are in the box. Then answer the question at the bottom of the page.

jeans	bee	wheel	jeep
meal	tree	sheep	stream

What will Jean do?

Jean will eat the m ____ ____ l.

The Great Big Book of Fun Phonics Activities © Scholastic Professional Books

Name _____

Crossword Puzzle

Look at each picture clue. Read the words in the box.
Write each picture name in the puzzle.

sheep	leaf	steam
wheel	jeep	jeans

Across

2.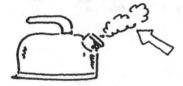

4.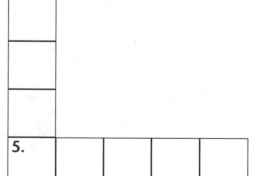

5.

Down

1.

3.

4.

Digraphs **ea, ee**

The Great Big Book of Fun Phonics Activities © Scholastic Professional Books

Name _____

Riddle in the Middle

What falls but never gets broken?

Find the name of each picture in the word box. Write the word on the lines. Put one letter on each line. Now find the answer to the riddle. Read the letters in the tall box from top to bottom. Write the answer.

pail	clay	chain	tray

1.

1. ___ ___ ___ ___

2.

2. ___ ___ ___ ___

3.

3. ___ ___ ___ ___

4.  4. ___ ___ ___ ___ ___

Answer: _____ .

Name _____

Use Those Clues!

Read each clue. Draw a line to the picture that matches it. Write the word.

1. It is on your foot.

   It is a _____.

pie

2. A man can put it on.

   It is a _____.

hoe

3. You can eat this.

   It is a _____.

toe

4. You can dig with this.

   It is a _____.

tie

The Great Big Book of Fun Phonics Activities © Scholastic Professional Books

Name _____

Where Did the Ball Go?

The soccer team is looking for its ball. You can find it
in the picture. Color shapes with long **e** words blue.
Color shapes with long **i** and long **o** words red. Color
shapes with long **a** words yellow.

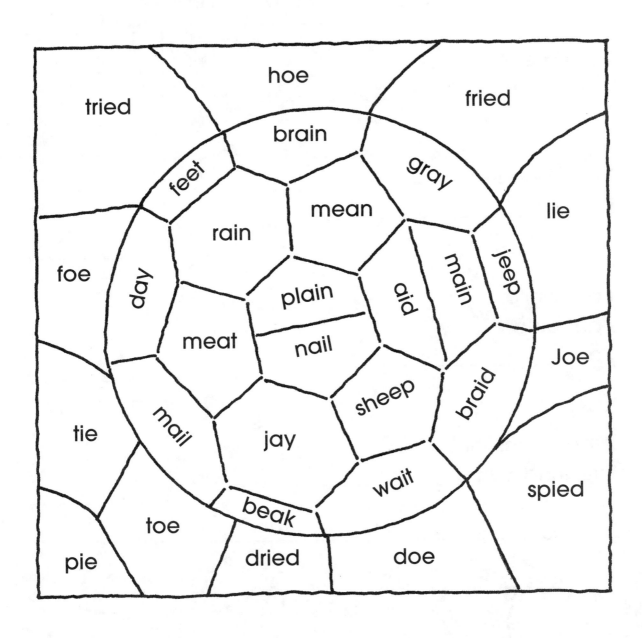

Name _____

Picture This!

Read each riddle. Look at the pictures. Then cut and paste the picture that goes with each riddle. Write the word that completes each riddle. Use words from the box.

go	snow	blow	elbow

1. I am green.
   I tell you to _____.

2. I can bend.
   I am an _____.

3. I am white.
   I am cold.
   I am _____.

4. A boy does this.
   The wind can _____, too.

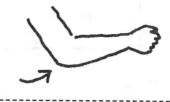

Long **o** Spelled **o, ow**

Name _____

Finish the Rhymes

Look at each picture. Then write the missing words to finish each rhyme. Use the words in the box.

float	coat	road	boat	toad	goat

1. The _____

   Sat by the _____.

2. Joan puts a _____

   On her baby _____.

3. Our little _____

   Will not _____!

Name _____

Round and Round

Look at the scene. Color the things that are hiding.
Their long **e** names are in the box. Then answer the
question at the bottom of the page. Use a word from
the box.

cherry	baby	bunny	puppy
monkey	key	daisy	penny

What pet can unlock a door?

A _____ !

Puzzle Rhymes

Look at each puzzle picture at the top of the page. Look for a puzzle picture with a name that rhymes at the bottom of the page. Cut and paste each puzzle piece to make a puzzle rhyme.

P O O L

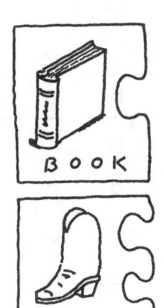

B O O K

M O O N

B O O T

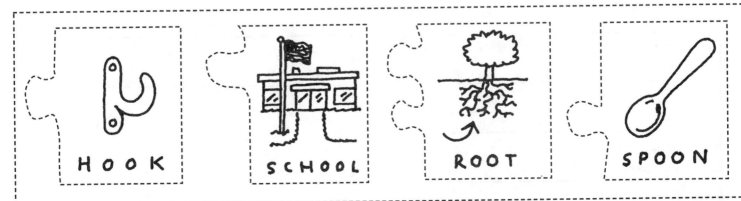

H O O K   S C H O O L   R O O T   S P O O N

Word Search

In this puzzle, find 4 more words that rhyme with 🔲. 
Find 3 words that rhyme with 🎎. Circle the words.
Then write the words on the lines.

l	o	o	k	o	p	o	x
o	x	o	c	s	y	t	b
b	o	r	o	p	r	o	k
o	s	h	o	o	k	o	o
o	t	g	k	o	k	k	x
w	o	o	d	h	o	o	k
s	t	o	o	d	o	o	i
o	o	d	o	p	p	o	o

book   **hood**

_____   _____

_____   _____

_____   _____

_____

The Great Big Book of Fun Phonics Activities © Scholastic Professional Books

Concentration

Cut out all the cards with a partner. Then play Concentration. Your teacher will tell you how to play the game.

 leaf	 steak	 break
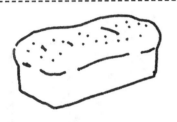 bread	 sweater	 head
 thread	 feather	 peach
 jeans	seal	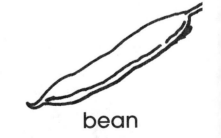 bean

Name _____

The Crawling Baby

Help the baby crawl to its mother. Follow the pictures
on the path whose **aw** names are in the box. Draw a
path for the baby.

yawn	paw	fawn	saw
shawl	straw	draw	claw

Name _____

Find the Treasure

Play this game with a partner. Who will get to the treasure first? Your teacher will tell you how to play.

Name _____

Show What You Know

Look at the picture that begins each row. Fill in the circle next to the word that matches the picture.

1. ○ jacks   ○ jeans   ○ gate

2. ○ bell   ○ boot   ○ ball

3. ○ sheep   ○ green   ○ book

4. ○ wheel   ○ hook   ○ book

5. ○ well   ○ clock   ○ nail

6. ○ steak   ○ sweater   ○ stop

7. ○ baby   ○ penny   ○ cherry

8. ○ snow   ○ boat   ○ bowl

9. ○ tray   ○ blow   ○ rainbow

10. ○ toad   ○ toast   ○ book

11. ○ tie   ○ pail   ○ pie

12. ○ bow   ○ toe   ○ train

The Great Big Book of Fun Phonics Activities © Scholastic Professional Books

A Book of Riddles

What do you call a ball that has feet?

A football.

Who would win a race, a potato or a cabbage?

A cabbage, because it is a head.

What do you call a baseball team that is asleep?

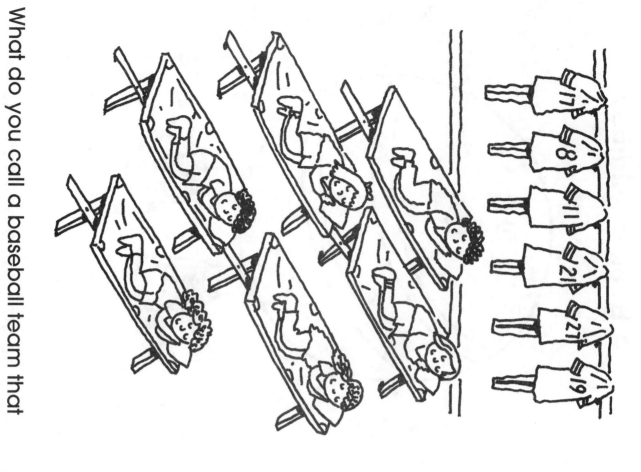

A dream team.

What do you call swimming lessons?

Pool school.

Classroom Fun ....

Vowel Digraphs

Digraph Hats

Arrange six children in a circle, each facing the other's back, and put a hat on the head of one child. Tell this child to take off the hat and put it on the head of the next child as you read a list of words. Ask children to listen for a word that has a certain digraph and when they hear you say it, to stop passing the hat. For example, if children are listening for a word with an *ea* digraph, as in *peach*, you might say, "boot, row, coast, sheep, mail, *jeans*." The person with the hat leaves the circle, and the game continues. When there are only two children left, they stand face to face, moving the hat back and forth quickly. The child left *not* wearing the hat is the winner.

Digraph Scavenger Hunt

Divide the class into four groups, one each for long *a*, long *e*, long *o*, and one for the long and short sounds of *oo*. Tell children they will be going on a scavenger hunt for things whose names have these vowel digraphs. Have each group first brainstorm a list of items they can look for. Then, give groups about 10 minutes to find objects in the classroom. Let the game continue throughout the day (perhaps on the playground, in the cafeteria, and so on). Have the groups "show and tell" at the end of the day.

Ring-Around-a-Digraph

To play this game with a large group, have children hold hands in two concentric rings facing one another. Put the same number of children in each ring (those in the outer ring will stretch their arms farther). Give each player a word that contains a digraph. Use exactly the same list of digraphs for both "rings" to ensure that each child will find a match. Then have the rings parade in opposite directions until you say "Stop." Each pair of adjoining children tells each other their words. If the words have the same digraph with the same pronunciation (for example, *goat/road, trail/rain, play/pay*), the two leave the ring and go to a winners' area. The game is over when everyone has "won."

Classroom Fun

Write a Funny Story

Tell children they will write a funny story using words they have learned in this book. Duplicate the Story Shapes Patterns on page 237 and fill in the word choices shown below. Then distribute the patterns to children. Without disclosing the story below, have them circle one thing from each shape. Then write this story frame on chart paper or reproduce it for children, leaving long blanks for children to fill in:

Once upon a time there was a ❶ _____
🔺 _____ . One day the 🔺_____
looked ▪3 _____ . There was a
❹ _____ ! "Will you be my pet?"
the 🔺 _____ asked. I will feed you
⭐ _____ . You can sleep ◆ _____ .
"Okay," said the ❹ _____ and it came
inside. And the 🔺 _____ and the
❹ _____ are both happy to this very day.

❶
happy
sad
lucky
sleepy
small
tall

🔺
queen
baby
cook
football team
man named Mr. Clay

▪3
out on the back lawn
on a train
in the woods
in a pail
in a haystack

❹
monkey
bunny
puppy
snail
seal
sheep

⭐
cherry pie and steak
bread and cream
wheat toast and jam
a bowl of green beans

◆
in a tree
in a haystack
in the bedroom
at the zoo
at school

Children will enjoy illustrating their stories. Have children take turns reading their stories to their classmates from an "author's chair" and sharing their illustrations. Use the story shapes patterns again with new lists of words as your class goes on to other phonics elements.

Words in a Box

On index cards, write about ten one-syllable words with vowel digraphs, and cut them in two. The first part should be the beginning consonant sound or sounds, and the second part should be the vowel and any ending sound or sounds. Put the first-part cards in one box and the second-part cards in another box. Have children take turns choosing a card from each box and putting the cards together to see if they make a word. As children make words, have them write the words in a list under their name. If the child cannot make a word, the next child takes a turn. Keep returning cards to the appropriate box after each turn. The child with the longest list wins.

st eam   sh oot

Make a Word Chain

Challenge children to make a word chain that is as long as possible within a certain time limit. Begin the chain by writing a word such as *seat* on the chalkboard. Invite children to change one letter at a time to make a new word. They can exchange a letter, drop a letter, or add a letter. For example, you might have a chain that looks like this:

*seat, **m**eat, *meal*, **s**eal, *seam*, *steam*, *team*, **b**eam*

Have children work in teams. Give one point for each word the team makes and two points for each word that has a vowel digraph.

Word and Picture Card Sort

Invite small groups of children to use the Word Cards and Picture Cards on pages 238–239 for sorting. First, have children sort the Picture Cards according to vowel sounds (long *a*, long *e*, long *o*, long *i*, short and long *oo*, short *e*, and the sound of *aw*). Then have them sort the Word Cards according to spelling (noting that *steak*, *bread*, and *leaf* have the same *ea* spelling but different vowel sounds). Encourage children to come up with other ways to sort the cards, such as by beginning sounds, ending sounds, and so on.

Riddle Fun

Write words with vowel digraphs on small slips of paper and place the slips in a can or bag. Have children take turns choosing a word and creating riddle clues for the word. Encourage them to think of clues for word meaning as well as the way the word sounds. Have them give their hardest clue first, then an easier one, until the class guesses the word. Model the first riddle for them, pausing after each clue: "This is an animal. It is a baby horse. Its name begins with an *f*. It ends in *l*. It has the long *o* sound." *(foal)* As children try to come up with their own clues, prompt them when necessary.

Freeze Spelling

Give children large cards, some with vowel digraphs (*ea, ai, ea, ee, oa, oo, o, ow, ay, ie, all, aw, oe*), and some with consonants that stand for beginning and ending consonant sounds

(*t, l, c, sp, k, d, p, t, st, m, n, cl, tr, sn, sp, sh, ch*). Have children mingle, finding out what letters and letter combinations are available. Then, say "Start!" and have children find at least two other children that have letters that make a word. When a group of children make a word, have them shout "Word!" Then have the entire class "freeze" until the group spells its word as you write it on the chalkboard. See how many words the class can make in a ten-minute period.

What Did I Say?

Many children love to find mistakes. Your class can have fun correcting intentional errors that you generate. Write sentences on the chalkboard with mistakes involving words with digraphs, and invite children to correct them. For example:

Every night you brush your *jeep*. *(teeth)*
Ice cream tastes *clean*. *(sweet)*
A king is married to a *bean*. *(queen)*
Dad cuts the grass on the *street*. *(lawn)*

Instant Activities

Silent Letters To help children see how the second letter is silent in vowel pairs like *ai, ay, ea, ee, oa, oe,* and *ie,* write words like *rain, day, bean, bee, road, toe,* and *tie* on the chalkboard. For each word, have children circle the vowel whose name can be heard and underline the silent letter.

Bean Toss Write different vowel digraphs on slips of paper and place each slip in a cup of a muffin tin. Have children take turns tossing a bean into the muffin tin. They must then say a word that has the vowel digraph written on the slip in the cup where their bean landed.

Alike or Different? Say word pairs like the ones below, one at a time, and have children raise their hands if the words have the same vowel sound: *wheel/sleep, pail/road, he/me, brain/sail, cheap/tray, blow/row, coach/float, moon/food, crook/croak.*

Make a Word Write the vowel pairs *ee, ea, oo, oa,* and *ai* in columns on chart paper or on the chalkboard. Challenge children to make as many words as they can from each digraph by adding consonants or consonant blends before or after the vowel pair.

Missing Letters Write these mystery words and have children add a vowel digraph that completes each one: *sw_ _t (sweet, sweat); m_ _n (moon, mean, main); ch_ _n (chain); gr_ _(grow, gray); bl_ _(blow); j_ _p (jeep); st_ _l (steal, steel, stool); sp_ _k (speak); s_ _k (seek, soak).* Have children use each word they form in a sentence.

Only Digraphs, Please! Write words with short vowels, such as *pin, red, men, cot,* and *lap* on the chalkboard. Invite children to make a new word by adding another vowel to the word, creating a digraph. *(pain, read, mean, coat, leap)*

Bag Words Place the Word Cards from page 238 in a bag. Have children take turns choosing three words and using all three in a sentence. Encourage silliness. For example: *The* baby *ate* hay *out of a* bowl.

Sound of the Day Declare each day a vowel sound day, such as Long *a* Day. Hang a large piece of paper on the wall, and have children write words or draw pictures whose names have digraphs that make the long *a* sound. At the end of the day, read aloud all the words. Repeat with long *o*, long *e*, short *oo*, long *oo*, and the sound *aw*.

Story Shapes Patterns

1.

2.

3.

4.

5.

6.

Word Cards

nail	tray	leaf	tree
key	toe	tie	coat
book	pool	bowl	baby
bread	break	ball	draw

Picture Cards

Word Bank

Below is a list of words that you may use to illustrate words with vowel digraphs. Some of these words are included in the Word/Picture Card set on pages 238–239. Ideas for using these cards and additional cards you may create yourself can be found in "Classroom Fun," pages 233–235.

Vowel Digraphs

ai
braid
brain
chain
rain
train

aw
draw
jaw
paw
saw
straw

ay
day
gray
jay
pay
play

e
be
he
me
she
we

ea (long e)
clean
cream
meat
read
speak

ea (short e)
bread
breath
head
steady
sweater

ea (long a)
break
great
steak

ee
cheek
deep
screen
seed
sheet

ey
key
money
monkey
valley

ie
fried
pie
tie

o
go
no
so

oa
coach
coast
goal
soak
throat

oe
doe
hoe
toe

oo (short)
crook
good
shook
stood
wool

oo (long)
cool
food
hoop
shoot
zoo

ow
bowl
know
show
slow
snow

y (long e)
funny
happy
lucky
rocky
sleepy

Teacher Notes

Page 216 See page 214, "Working with the Poem."

Page 217 *Answers:* jeans, tree, wheel, bee, jeep, sheep, meal, stream; meal.

Page 218 *Answers:* Across: 2. wheel 4. jeep 5. steam. Down: 1. sheep (given) 3. leaf 4. jeans.

Page 219 *Answers:* 1. tray 2. clay 3. pail 4. chain. *R*iddle *answer:* rain.

Page 220 *Answers:* 1. toe 2. tie 3. pie 4. hoe.

Page 221 *Answers:* **blue:** feet, mean, meat, jeep, sheep, beak; **red:** tried, hoe, fried, lie, Joe, spied, doe, dried, pie, tie, toe, foe; **yellow:** day, rain, brain, gray, play, nail, main, aid, braid, jay, mail, wait.

Page 222 *Answers:* 1. go 2. elbow 3. snow 4. blow.

Page 223 *Answers:* 1. toad, road 2. coat, goat 3. boat, float.

Page 224 *Preparation:* Emphasize the long *e* sound in the second syllable, as you read aloud the words in the box to help children focus on the pictures they are looking for. *Answers:* cherry, baby, bunny, puppy, daisy, monkey, key. *Riddle answer:* mon**key**.

Page 225 *Answers:* pool/school, book/hook, moon/spoon, boot/root.

Page 226 *Answers:* shook (given), look, cook, took, hook; good, wood, stood.

Page 227 *Game Directions:* Have children mix the cards and turn them face down. The first player turns two cards face up. The player says both words out loud. If the words have the same vowel sound, the player keeps them and takes another turn. If not, cards must be turned face down and the other player takes a turn. The game is over when the children have picked up all the cards.
Answers: Long *e*: leaf, peach, jeans, seal, bean.
Long *a*: steak, break.
Short *e*: bread, sweater, head, thread, feather.

Page 228 *Answers:* yawn, paw, draw, saw, straw, claw, shawl, fawn.

Page 229 *Game Directions:* Players take turns rolling a number cube, moving that number of spaces, and saying the word in the space. To stay there, the player must then say another word with the same vowel sound or return to the previous location. The first player to reach the treasure wins.

Page 230 *Answers:* Children will fill in the circle next to the appropriate word. 1. jeans 2. boot 3. sheep 4. hook 5. nail 6. sweater 7. baby 8. bowl 9. tray 10. toad 11. pie 12. toe.

Vowel Diphthongs

Using This Book

Classroom Management

Reproducibles Reproducible pages 245–247 offer a variety of individual and partner activities. *Answers* or *Game* Directions appear as necessary in the *Teacher Notes* section on page 268.

Directions You may wish to go over the directions with children and verify that they can identify all picture cues before they begin independent work.

Games When children play partner games, circulate to make sure children understand procedures.

Working with the Poem

A poem on page 244 introduces the phonics element in this book, vowel diphthongs. Read this page aloud to children. Duplicate the poem so that children can work with it in a variety of ways:

Personal Response Read the poem aloud. Ask the children if they expected the poem's ending.

Phonemic Awareness Read the poem aloud and have children listen for a particular diphthong. For example, ask children to raise their hands when they hear a word that has the same vowel sound as *how*.

Sound to Letter Write the poem on chart paper or on the chalkboard, and have children circle words with diphthongs. Make word cards for words with diphthongs. Have children match the word cards to the words in the poem.

Innovation Brainstorm ideas first. Then write the last two lines of the poem on chart paper, leaving blanks for the words *soil, oil,* and *ground*.

Connecting School and Home

The Family Letter on page 243 can be sent home to encourage families to reinforce what children are learning. Children will also enjoy sharing the Take-Home Book on pages 258–259. You can cut and fold these booklets ahead of time, or invite children to participate in the process. You might mount the pages on heavier stock so that you can place the Take-Home Book in your classroom library.

Word/Picture Card Sets

Pages 266–267 of this book contain matching sets of Word/Picture Cards drawn from the vocabulary presented in this book. You might mount these on heavier stock as a classroom resource. You might also duplicate and distribute them to children for use in matching and sorting activities. Each child can use a large envelope to store the cards.

Assessment

Page 258, Show What You Know, provides children with targeted practice in standardized test-taking skills, using the content presented in this book in the assessment items.

Dear Family,

In school your child is learning about vowel diphthongs. In a diphthong, two vowel letters make a sound that glides from one vowel sound to another. Some diphthongs are *ou* as in *round* and *ow* as in *down*.

mou**se**　　　**c**oi**n**　　　**b**oy

You may enjoy sharing some or all of these activities with your child:

Make Words with Clay
Use homemade or store-bought clay to form letters and then make words. You and your child might want to use one color for the diphthongs and another color for all the other letters.

Illustrate Words
Together with your child, draw illustrations for these words: *cow, mouse, flowers, crown, boy*. Then help your child label the pictures.

Reading Together
To practice reading words with diphthongs, look through your child's Take-Home Book, "Brownie." Ask your child to circle or underline all the words with diphthongs.

You may also wish to look for the following books in your local library:

Sincerely,

The Bremen Town Musicians

by Hans Wilhelm

Mouse Tales

by Arnold Lobel

Name _____

Toy Brown Mouse

Roy was a toy,
A toy brown mouse.
He made noise and dug
Down under the house.
Roy shouted loudly!
Now what had he found?
Deep in the soil —
Gold coins in the ground!

The Great Big Book of Fun Phonics Activities © Scholastic Professional Books

Name _____

Hide the Bones

Help the hound hide six bones. Cut out the bones.
Find the mounds with the same vowel sound
as **hound**. Paste a bone over each one.
Then finish the sentence.

cloud

sound

coin

out

found

boat

toy

mouse

hook

house

The h ____ ____ nd put six bones in the gr ____ ____ nd.

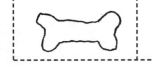

Name _____

Mystery Word

What do you do when you want someone to hear you?

Find the name of each picture in the word box.
Write the word on the lines. Put one letter on each line.
Now find the mystery word. Read the letters in the tall box from top to bottom. Write the mystery word.

| bounce | mouse | mouth | house | ground |

1. 1. _ _ _ _ _

2. 2. _ _ _ _ _

3. 3. _ _ _ _ _ _

4. 4. _ _ _ _ _ _

5. 5. _ _ _ _ _

Answer: _____.

The Great Big Book of Fun Phonics Activities © Scholastic Professional Books

Help the Owl

An owl can see almost everything. But this owl does not see the things named in the box. Circle the **ow** pictures to help the owl. Then color the scene.

cow	plow	gown	clown	crown

Name _____

Going Down to Town

Help the bus get to town. Write one of these words in the blank beside each picture name.

| tower | cow | down | crown | owl | clown |

Name _____

Riddle Rhymes

Read each riddle. Cut and paste the picture that
answers the riddle. Then write the answer.

1. It rhymes with .
   It is a small animal.

   It is a _____ .

2. It rhymes with .
   It is funny.

   It is a _____ .

3. It rhymes with .
   It makes milk for you.

   It is a _____ .

4. It rhymes with .
   It is on a sad face.

   It is a _____ .

Words That Talk

Some words sound like what they mean. Look at the cartoon. Complete the words that stand for sounds the animals are making. Use words from the box.

Pow	Growl	Yow	Meow	Ouch	Wow

Act out this cartoon. Then draw your own cartoon.

The Great Big Book of Fun Phonics Activities © Scholastic Professional Books

Name _____

The Joyville Train

Parts of the train track are missing! Read the clues.
Cut out the puzzle pieces. Paste the pieces on the
track so the train can get to Joyville.

This is a
name.

It is not
a girl.

You play
with this.

He rides
a horse.

It means
you have
fun.

JOYVILLE

boy

enjoy

Roy

cowboy

toy

Word Search

Circle these words that end in **oy**. They can go down or across. Then write the words.

| cowboy | enjoy | toy | boy | joy | annoy |

W J Y O Y O E

A O T O Y O N

J Y O T O U J

C O L P Q Y O

B C O W B O Y

N Y Y A O Y O

A N N O Y O P

_____

_____

_____

_____

_____

The Great Big Book of Fun Phonics Activities © Scholastic Professional Books

Name _____

Join the Club

Climb the steps to join the **oi** club. Cut out the **oi** word cards. Match each word card to a step. Paste the word card on the step. Then write each **oi** word on the tree.

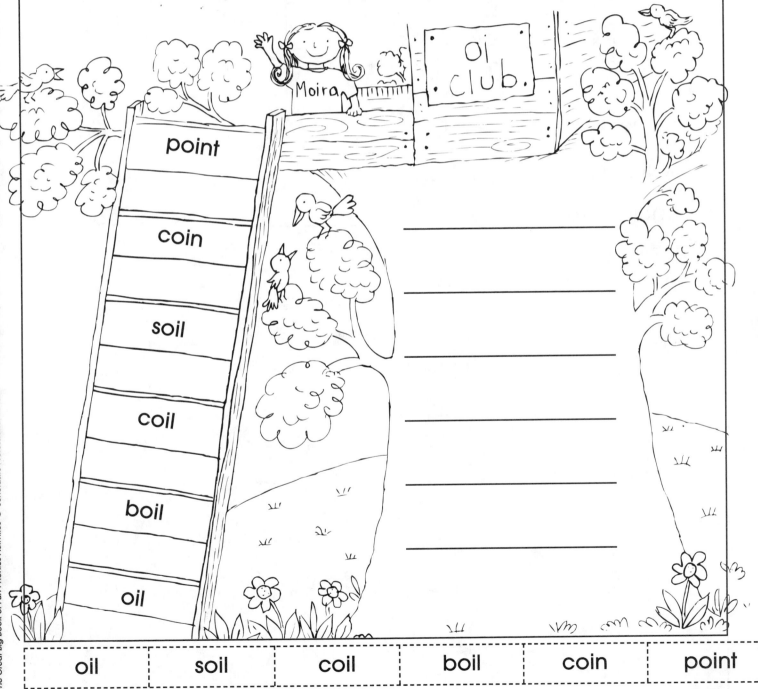

| oil | soil | coil | boil | coin | point |

Use the Code!

Look at the code below. Use it to figure out the words.
Write the words to complete the secret story.

□	☆	○	✪	△	◇	▯	⊙	△̇	⊞
b	c	f	o	i	s	l	p	n	t

Uncle Sam wants tea. I □✪△▯ _____ the

water. I put ○✪△▯ _____ on the tray.

Uncle Sam ⊙✪△△̇⊞◇_____ to my ear.

He finds a ☆✪△△̇ _____ there!

Name _____

Crossword Fun

Look at each picture clue. Read the words in the box.
Write each picture name in the puzzle.

| boy | coin | point | cowboy | noise | toy |

Across

3.

5.

6.

Down

1.

2.

4.

Puzzle Clues

Read each clue. Find the puzzle piece with the answer. Cut out each puzzle piece picture and paste it where it fits.

1. He has only this many.

new

2. You can eat this.

mew

3. A baby kitten says this.

stew

4. She just got this.

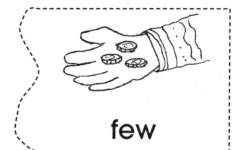

few

Name _____

The Way to Cowboy Town

Help the cowboy ride to Cowboy Town. Your teacher will tell you how to play this game.

Show What You Know

Look at the picture that begins each row.
Fill in the circle next to the word that matches
the picture.

1.   ○ horse ○ cow ○ cowboy

2.   ○ cow ○ cloud ○ clown

3.   ○ mouse ○ house ○ man

4.   ○ cake ○ coin ○ join

5.   ○ noise ○ note ○ now

6.   ○ plane ○ towel ○ plow

7.   ○ cloud ○ clown ○ crown

8. ○ tie ○ toy ○ boy

9. ○ cow ○ clown ○ coin

10. ○ nine ○ not ○ new

The Great Big Book of Fun Phonics Activities © Scholastic Professional Books

Brownie

Brownie found a towel in town.
Dad said, "Brownie, put that down."

Now Brownie has a brand new toy.
He can always count on Joy!

Brownie got a nice round ball.
Mom said, "No bouncing in the hall."

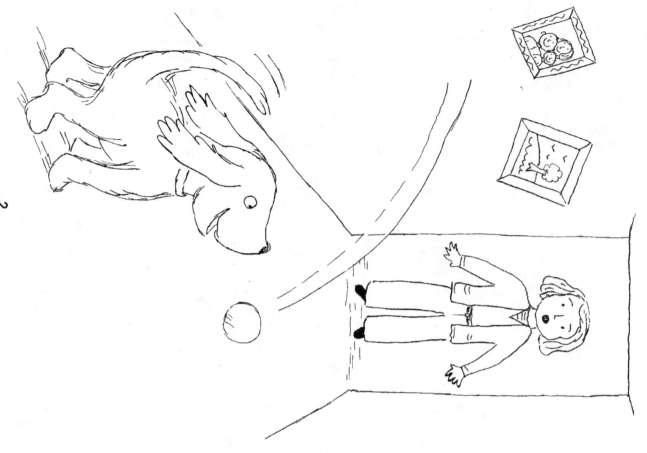

Brownie howled at all the boys.
Floyd said, "Brownie, stop that noise!"

Classroom Fun .....

Vowel Diphthongs

"Pick and Poke" Diphthongs

Play a "Pick and Poke" game to find out how well partners or individuals can distinguish between diphthongs. Make cards for the game by duplicating the pattern on page 265 or by using actual 3"x 5" index cards. Along the side of the card, punch five holes and write a diphthong beside each hole. Paste or draw a picture of a word that has a diphthong on the front of the card, as shown below. To make the game self-checking, turn the card over and put the word "yes" by the hole that corresponds to the correct diphthong. To use the card, children look at the picture and pick the diphthong they hear. They poke a pencil through the hole they picked and look at the back side. If they are correct, the pencil is poking through the "yes" hole.

Partners can play by taking turns and checking each other. They sit facing each other. When one child pokes an answer, the partner can see the "yes" and tell them if they are right.

Indoor Diphthong Scavenger Hunt

Invite groups of children to work together in a scavenger hunt. Reproduce the list below for each group. Tell children that this list is unusual—some of the items require that they use their imaginations. Explain that they have 15 minutes to collect, draw, or invent items mentioned on the list. Items that have been drawn or invented must be approved by the class before they can be checked off. The group with the most approved items wins.

- ❏ A house for a mouse
- ❏ Something that will not spoil
- ❏ Something that can bounce
- ❏ Something the class enjoys
- ❏ Something with a point
- ❏ Something that boils
- ❏ A toy
- ❏ Something you can chew
- ❏ Something that grew
- ❏ Something that makes you frown
- ❏ Something that is new
- ❏ Something a clown likes
- ❏ Something that is brown
- ❏ Something that makes a loud noise
- ❏ A coin
- ❏ Something that makes a soft sound
- ❏ Something round
- ❏ Something that comes from a cow

Classroom Fun

Tape It Up

Write four or five words with diphthongs in a column on chart paper, leaving plenty of room beside each word for letter dashes. Write the same words in big letters on index cards, and cut the words up, letter by letter. Lay the letters face down on a desk or table and place a tape dispenser there as well. Create teams of three or four children. Have teams take turns sending a member up to choose a letter, take a bit of tape, and place the letter on the chart next to one of the words you have written. Tell them to choose the space carefully in order to leave room for the other letters that will be needed to spell out the word completely. Encourage team members to help any child who is unsure of the placement of a letter. Each time a child puts the last letter in place to complete a word, that child's team gets a point.

Mouse or Clown?

Draw and label a mouse and a clown on drawing paper or poster board, leaving plenty of room above each figure. Then, cut out shapes of balloons from colored construction paper and put them in a box or envelope next to the poster. Tell children that *mouse* and *clown* have the same vowel sound but are spelled differently. Have a volunteer underline the *ou* and *ow* in each word. Invite children to come up during the day to write *ou* and *ow* words on each balloon and paste them over the mouse or the clown, depending on the spelling. Provide string so that children can connect a string from each balloon to the figure. At the end of the day, have children take turns reading the words on each bunch of balloons.

round   _____ _____ _____ [n] [d]

flew   _____ _____ _____ _____

toy   _____ [o] _____

owl   _____ _____ _____

town   [t] _____ _____ _____

Diphthong Concentration

Use the Word Cards or Picture Cards on pages 266–267 or other cards you have created to have pairs of children play Diphthong Concentration. Decide before each game whether children are to match words to pictures or match the same diphthongs occurring in different words. To begin play, lay the cards face down. Then have the pairs of children take turns turning over two cards at a time, looking for the match. If a child turns over two cards that match, he or she may keep the cards. If not, the cards must be turned face down again. Play then goes to the other child. When all the cards have been picked up, the player with the most cards wins.

Bag Words

On each of twelve index cards, write a word that has a diphthong. Cut each card in half just before the diphthong. Use words like those shown:

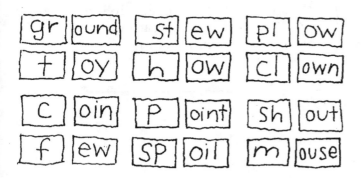

Put the word beginnings in one bag and the word endings in another. Then have children take turns choosing a beginning and ending sound. If the two cards make a word, the child may keep the two halves. If the child can make a sentence using the word or say a rhyming word, give out a prize, such as a sticker or a gold star. Continue until all the possible words have been made.

Find Your Partner

Write words like the following on large index cards. Read them aloud with children and talk about each word's meaning: *house, mouse, found, pound, round, boy, toy, joy, boil, spoil, brown, clown, crown, flew,* and *blew*. Cut the cards into two parts, cutting before the diphthong, and distribute the pieces randomly, one to each child. Have each child look for the child with the matching half of the card. Have pairs raise their hands jointly and read their word out loud. You may wish to cut the ends of the cards in puzzle piece shapes so children can be sure they are meant to go together.

Make Up a Silly Story

Brainstorm and write on the board a list of words with diphthongs. Then have children work with a partner to choose two or three of the words to make up a silly short story. Start them off by modeling this story for them using the words *new, enjoy,* and *trout.*

> Tracy the **Trout** wanted a treat. He decided to go shopping. He went to the store and tried on a **new** hat. "This is a nice hat," he thought. "I will **enjoy** wearing this hat!"

Children may dictate their stories, or just tell them orally to the class.

Instant Activities

Ow or Ou? Mark two bags with labels ou and ow. Write words like *brown, down, cloud, couch, cloud, found, about, house, out, mouth, shout,* and *owl* on cards. Have children say each word and put the card in the bag with the correct diphthong label.

Quick Riddles Invite children to make up riddles for words with *oy* and *oi*. For example: "This is something my mother does not like. I make too much of it. It is loud." *(noise)* Children can take turns standing in front of the class to tell their riddles.

Stand Up for Diphthongs Say these words aloud and have children stand up if the word has the diphthong *ow:* "bowl, *cow,* show, *now, gown,* blow, *frown,* snow, *out,* mow, *mouth,* grow, *clown, down.*"

Color the Letters Write words like these on the chalkboard: *dew, owl, spoil, ground.* Have volunteers take colored chalk and write over the letters that make the diphthong in each word.

Rhyming Words and Pictures Spread out the Word Cards and Picture Cards from pages 266–267 on a table. Hold up one card, and call on a child to come up and match it to another card. The match may be of a picture to a rhyming word or two words with the same diphthong.

Which Diphthong Was That? Give an index card to each child and have him or her write one of the five diphthongs on it. As you call out a word from the list on page 268, have children hold up their card if the word has the sound and spelling of their diphthong.

Noisy Words Say these words and have children make a noise by tapping or stomping their feet each time they hear a word with the diphthongs *oi* or *oy: coin, point, soil, shout, toy, out, boil, plow, enjoy, threw, cowboy.*

Pick and Poke Card Pattern

(front of card)

ou ○

ow ○

ew ○

oi ○

oy ○

Fold →

○

○

○

○

○

(back of card)

To create a Pick and Poke card:

1. Cut out card around outside edges.
2. Attach picture to front of the card.
3. Fold up back so that hole indicators match.
4. Staple or tape top and bottom edges together.
5. Punch holes through hole indicators.
6. Write *yes* on back next to correct diphthong.

Word Cards

house	mouse	boy	toy
coin	noise	owl	cow
plow	town	clown	crown
new	stew	cloud	couch

Picture Cards

Word Bank

Below is a list of words that you may use to illustrate words with vowel diphthongs. Some of these words are included in the Word/Picture Card set on pages 266–267. Ideas for using these cards and additional cards you may create yourself can be found in "Classroom Fun," pages 261–263.

─── **Vowel Diphthongs** ───

ou	**oy**	**oi**	**ow**	**ew**
blouse	annoy	boil	brown	blew
bounce	boy	coin	crown	chew
couch	cowboy	join	down	few
count	enjoy	moist	flower	flew
found	joy	noise	fowl	grew
ground	loyal	oil	frown	new
house	Roy	point	gown	news
loud	toy	soil	howl	stew
mouse		spoil	now	
mouth		toil	plow	
pound		voice	towel	
round			tower	
scout			vow	

Teacher Notes

Page 245 *Answers:* sound, cloud, found, out, house, mouse; ou—hound, ground.

Page 246 *Answers:* 1. mouse 2. house 3. ground 4. bounce 5. mouth.
Mystery word: shout.

Page 247 *Answers:* cow, plow, gown, clown, crown.

Page 248 *Answers:* down, tower, cow, owl, crown, clown.

Page 249 *Answers:* 1. mouse 2. clown 3. cow 4. frown.

Page 250 *Answers:* Frame 1: Yow!, Meow!, Growl!
Frame 2: Pow!, Ouch!
Frame 3: Wow!, Wow!, Wow!
Encourage children to draw similar cartoons and share them with the class.

Page 251 *Answers:* This is a name: Roy; It is not a girl: boy; You play with this: toy; He rides a horse: cowboy; It means you have fun: enjoy.

Page 252 *Answers:* enjoy, joy, toy, cowboy, boy, annoy.

Page 253 *Answers:* point, coin, soil, coil, boil, oil.

Page 254 *Answers:* 1. boil 2. foil 3. points 4. coin.

Page 255 *Answers:* Across: 3. cowboy 5. coin 6. toy;
Down: 1. point 2. boy 4. noise.

Page 256 *Answers:* 1. few 2. stew 3. mew 4. new.

Page 257 *Game Directions:* Have players take turns rolling a number cube and moving that many spaces. They say the name of the picture and say another word with the same diphthong. If they do, they can stay in the space. If not, they must return to their previous position. The first player to get to Cowboy Town wins.

Page 258 *Answers:* Children will fill in the circle next to the appropriate word. 1. cowboy 2. cloud 3. mouse 4. coin 5. noise 6. plow 7. clown 8. toy 9. cow 10. new.

Vowels With r

TREATS

Using This Book

Classroom Management

Reproducibles Reproducible pages 273–285 offer a variety of individual and partner activities. Simple directions to the children are augmented when necessary by *Answers* or *Game Directions* in the *Teacher Notes* section on page 296.

Directions You may wish to go over the directions with children and verify that they can identify all picture cues and read any words in the activities before they begin independent work.

Games When children play partner games, you may want to circulate in order to make sure children understand procedures.

Working with the Poem

A poem on page 272 introduces the phonics element in this book, vowels with *r*. Start by reading this page aloud to children. As children progress through the activities in this book, you may want to duplicate the poem so children can work with it in a variety of ways:

Personal Response Read the poem aloud and have children talk about it. Do they have special ways of keeping in touch with home?

Phonemic Awareness Read the poem aloud each day. Have children listen for the sound of a vowel with *r*, and ask them to raise their hands each time they hear one.

Sound to Letter Write the poem on a chart, and ask children to point to or circle words that include vowels with *r*.

Innovation Ask children to brainstorm ideas for new characters whose names contain a vowel with *r*. Encourage children to say new versions of the poem for the class.

Connecting School and Home

The Family Letter on page 271 can be sent home to encourage families to reinforce what children are learning. Children will also enjoy sharing the Take-Home Book on pages 287–288. You can cut and fold these booklets ahead of time, or invite children to participate in the process. You might also mount the pages on heavier stock so you can place the Take-Home Book in your classroom library.

Word/Picture Card Sets

Pages 294–295 of this book contain matching sets of Word/Picture Cards drawn from the vocabulary presented in this book. You might mount these on heavier stock as a classroom resource. You might also duplicate and distribute them to children for use in matching and sorting activities. Each child can use a large envelope to store the cards.

Assessment

Page 286, Show What You Know, provides children with targeted practice in standardized test-taking skills, using the content presented in this book in the assessment items.

Dear Family,

In school, your child is learning about vowels with *r*.

When a vowel comes before *r* in a word, the *r* "controls" the sound of the vowel. Some words with *r*-controlled vowels are *hear, twirl, horn,* and *burn*.

c**ar**   g**ir**l   ch**air**

You may enjoy sharing some or all of the following activities with your child:

Word Poster
Draw the outline of a picture of a car on white paper. Post it on the wall or on the refrigerator. Over the next few days, have your child add pictures or names of objects that end with *-ar*. Repeat for other vowels with *r* that your child is studying.

I Spy
When you are out walking, driving, or shopping with your child, play "I Spy." Tell your child you see something whose name has a vowel with *r* (for example, a porch, a bird, or a shopping cart). Have your child try to guess the item.

Reading Together
To practice reading words with *r*-controlled vowels, look over your child's Take-Home Book, "Do Your Best!" Ask your child to circle vowels with *r* and read those words to you. You may also wish to look for these books in your local library:

Sincerely,

The Missing Tarts
by B. G. Hennessey

The Old Red Rocking Chair
by Phyllis Root

Name _____

Sparky Sharky

Sparky Sharky
Had to wear
A horn when
He went anywhere.

His mom said,
"Sparky, don't go far.
I like to know
Just where you are!"

TOOT
TOOT

Name _____

Picture Match

What goes with what? Draw a line to match
each picture on the left to a picture on the right.
Write **ar** to finish each picture name. Then use one
of the names to answer the riddle.

1.     j _____ _____

2.     b _____ _____ n

3.    c _____ _____

4.     c _____ _____ ds

5.     c _____ _____ t

What do you have to start up every day? A _____ .

The Great Big Book of Fun Phonics Activities © Scholastic Professional Books

Vowels with **r: ar**   **273** •••

Name _____

Pictures in the Sky

Read the word next to each star. Connect the stars that have **ar** words. What animal can you see? Write its name to complete the sentence.

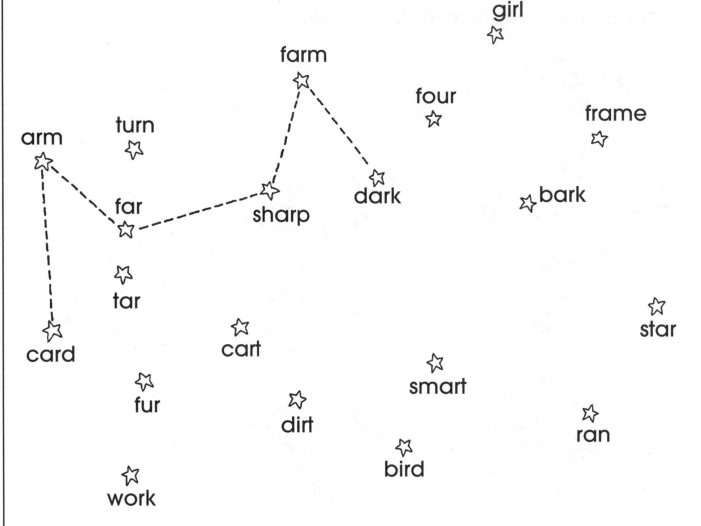

I am a sh _____ _____ k.

The Great Big Book of Fun Phonics Activities © Scholastic Professional Books

Name _____

A Thirsty Team

This team is thirsty! Help them get to the drinks. Write the name of each picture you see. Use all the words in the box.

girl	skirt	shirt	dirt	thirty	first

It's Too Silly!

Look at the silly pictures below. Write **ir** or **ar** to complete each word.

1. a sm __ __ t b __ __ d

2. a sh __ __ k that p __ __rks

3. a d __ __ ty st __ __

4. a c __ __ g __ __ den

Name _____

Purr-fect Crossword

Look at the pictures. Read the clues. Write each picture name in the puzzle. Use the words in the box.

| purr | nurse | fur | purse | burn |

Across

2. This keeps a dog warm.

4. She takes care of you.

5. This is what fire can do.

Down

1. You keep money here.

3. Happy cats do this.

Dessert at Gertie's

Let's have dessert! Look at the scene. Write **er** to finish each word. Then read what each person is saying.

I am the cl ___ ___ k. May I s ___ ___ ve you?

Nice f ___ ___ n!

Tell h ___ ___ what you want.

This is p ___ ___ fect!

The Great Big Book of Fun Phonics Activities © Scholastic Professional Books

Name _____

Home Run!

Help the batter get to home plate! Your teacher will tell you how to play this game.

fur

curl

part

chart

thorn

fort

shark

clerk

her

burn

Read a word. Say a sentence. Move 3.

Read a word. Move 2.

Read a word. Move 1.

Rest here.

Read a word. Say a rhyme. Move 2.

Rest here.

Read a word. Go back 1.

Rest here.

Read a word. Go back 1.

Go back 2.

Read a word. Move 2.

HOME

Move back 3.

Go back to home.

Rest here.

Rest here.

Go ahead 2.

Read a word. Say a sentence. Move 3.

Rest here.

Go back 1.

nurse

spark

storm

short

sharp

Puzzle Me!

Make words that end with **-air**. Find the matches. Cut and paste them to make the word that names the picture on the right.

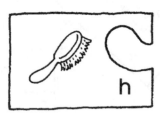
ch

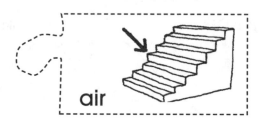
air

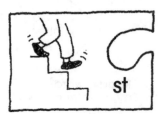
p

air

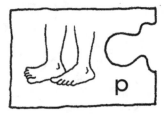
st

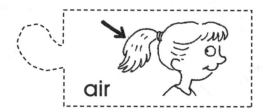
air

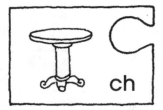
h

air

f

air

Name _____

Riddle, Riddle

Read each riddle. Cut and paste the picture that answers each riddle. Then write the answer. You will use words from the box.

Dear	tear	ear	year	gear

1. I have 365 days.
    I have four seasons.
    I am a _____.

2. I am on your head.
    I help you hear.
    I am an _____.

3. I start your letters.
    I come before a name.
    I am the word _____.

4. I am on your bike.
    I help the wheels turn.
    I am the _____.

5. If you are sad, you cry me.
    I come from your eye.
    I am a _____.

What Is It?

Color all the boxes that have words that end with **are** and rhyme with **care**. What do you see? Complete the sentence. Use one of the words you colored.

fern	there	bark	fur	oar
barn	☆ share	fare	☆ care	wore
pair	☆ dare	☆ square	☆ mare	arm
harp	☆ spare	hare	☆ scare	tear
yard	bear	farm	far	art
purr	her	ear	bird	jar

It is a _____ kite.

The Great Big Book of Fun Phonics Activities © Scholastic Professional Books

Name _____

Word Ladders

Follow the directions to make new words. Write each new word on its word ladder. Then, cut and paste the matching pictures next to each word.

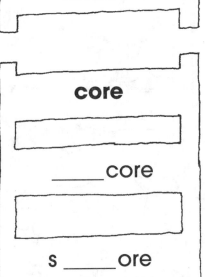

fire

_____ire

_____ire

1. Change the **f** to **t**.

2. Change the **t** to **w**.

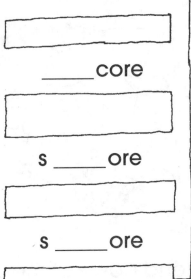

core

_____core

s _____ore

s _____ore

3. Add an **s**.

4. Change the **c** to **t**.

5. Change the **t** to **h**.

At the Fair!

Claire and Bert are at the fair. But there are some things they can not see! Color the pictures whose names are in the word box. Then answer the riddle.

| square | horse | core | chair | stairs | fire | tire |

What goes up and down at the same time?

_____

Vowels With r: air, ear, are, ire, ore

The Great Big Book of Fun Phonics Activities © Scholastic Professional Books

Name _____

Word Square

Circle these words that have vowels with **r**.
They go across or down. Then write the words.

| bird | chair | hair | hear | shark | square | turn |

s   q   u   a   r   e   b   _____

c   f   f   y   s   c   x   _____

h   w   c   j   h   q   y   _____

a   f   h   e   a   r   b   _____

i   u   a   q   r   k   i   _____

r   x   i   s   k   i   r   _____

t   u   r   n   q   w   d   _____

Show What You Know

Look at the picture in each row. Fill in the circle next to the word with the same vowel with **r** sound as the name of the picture.

1.   ○ stairs ○ car ○ store

2.   ○ hair ○ chart ○ shirt

3.   ○ purse ○ horse ○ card

4.   ○ core ○ skirt ○ shell

5.   ○ gate ○ bird ○ goat

6.   ○ shark ○ tire ○ gear

7.   ○ jar ○ share ○ store

8.   ○ tire ○ wear ○ hair

9.   ○ large ○ barn ○ stork

10. ○ near ○ care ○ shore

The Great Big Book of Fun Phonics Activities © Scholastic Professional Books

Do Your Best!

HOME 3
VISITOR 4

Marcie had the last turn.
The score was 3 to 4.
Marcie stared at the dirt.

HOME 5
VISITOR 4

WHACK! Marcie hit the ball hard.
It went far, far out of the park.
Marcie did her best, and the score
was 5 to 4!

There was one girl on first base.
Everyone in the park was yelling.
Marcie was scared.

Marcie could hear her mom call,
"Just do your best, dear."
Marcie perked up.

Classroom Fun .....

Vowels With r

Flappable Fun Pictionary

Invite children to draw pictures of words that have vowels with *r*. You may want to post words from the Word Bank on page 296 as a resource. Then have children cut out each picture, leaving room above each picture so that the top edge can be folded under and pasted down, making the picture into a lift-up flap. Then have them arrange the flaps on pieces of tagboard or sturdy construction paper, pasting the top edge down. Have children take turns lifting up each picture and writing the name of each one under the picture. Bind children's Flappable Pictionary pages together into a book.

Where's That Sound?

Give each child in the classroom a slip of paper with one of these names written on it: *bird, car, horse, storm, turkey,* and *horn.* Tell them to sit down and not show anyone what is written on their paper. When you say "Start," children should stand and begin quietly making the sound that their object makes. They should walk around trying to find other classmates who are making that same sound. After a minute or two, tell everyone to sit where they are and see which group has found the most members.

Word Slides

Use the patterns and word strips on page 293 to help children recognize rhyming words with *r*-controlled vowel phonograms. (You may wish to mount the drawings on tagboard or poster board for durability.) Cut the strips apart and cut the slits through each pattern. Match the strip number to the pattern (strip 1 goes with the star, strip 2 with the chair). Then let children take turns sliding the beginning consonant sounds through the strips and reading each word. Challenge children to use each new word in a sentence.

Read the Footprints

Divide the class into teams and appoint one member of each "the walker." Give each group 10 paper footprints. Assign each group an *r*-controlled vowel, such as *or, ar,* or *ur.* When you say "Start," have the group write a word with the *r*-controlled vowel on one of the footprints and tape it to the floor. The walker may then advance one step. The first group to advance ten steps wins!

Classroom Fun

TV Quiz Game

To work on the meanings of words with r-controlled vowels, play a quiz game with children. Make a gameboard like the one below, with three pockets to hold questions on cards that fit into categories of difficulty—10 points for easy questions, 20 points for harder ones, and 30 points for the hardest. Write questions like the ones to the right on index cards. Place the questions in the pockets and divide the class into teams. Have teams take turns answering the questions, choosing questions of different difficulty. Encourage teams to work together to make up new questions that use vowels with r.

A Farm Mural

Talk with children about what a mural about a farm might show. Make a list of children's suggestions and record them on the chalkboard. Make sure they include things with r-controlled vowels, such as: a *turkey*, the farmer's *car*, a *barn*, a *yard*, a *cart*, *garden*, a *mare*, a *herd* of cows, *dirt* in the chicken yard, a *horse*, a *corn* field, *porch* on the farmer's house, and a *tractor*. Then, have a small group work together to create this mural, including only the objects whose names have vowels with r. After children complete the illustrations, have them label each picture. Then have them fill in the farm mural with any pictures they like that relate to a farm.

---

10 points (easy)

Name three *sports*.
What word rhymes with *ear*?
Name a *park* near you.
Name three animals that live on a *farm*.
How many *chairs* are in this room?
Where does a *shark* live?

---

20 points (medium difficulty)

Name three kinds of *birds*.
How many days are in a *year*?
How do you draw a *star*?
Name an animal that has *fur*.
Name a fruit that is *purple*.

---

30 points (challenging)

What can you make with *corn* meal?
Name a famous *fort*.
What kind of animals form a *herd*?

Mystery Messages

Write this mystery message on the chalkboard and have children fill in the blanks with *ir, er, ur, or,* or *ar* to make the message make sense:

> M_ _k will p_ _ k his c_ _ in the back y_ _d bef_ _e the st_ _m st_ _ts. (Mark will park his car in the back yard before the storm starts).

Depending on ability level, challenge children to write their own mystery words or sentences. (For example, some children can write just one word and draw a picture as a clue; others can write a complete sentence.) Have children write the answer on the back of each paper. Encourage children to exchange mystery words and sentences with a partner.

Personality Scavenger Hunt

Divide children into teams. Challenge the groups to go on a personality scavenger hunt. Give out a list like the one below, and challenge each team to find someone in the classroom who has each characteristic on the list. Tell children to write the person's name beside the characteristic. Use characteristics that involve *r*-controlled vowels, like these:

- has a purse
- likes turkey
- is wearing something purple
- has a pair of sneakers
- is wearing a skirt or a shirt
- has curly hair
- has a part in his or her hair
- has a warm coat
- has a scarf
- plays sports
- has been to the circus
- has been to the seashore
- has a pet turtle at home

Children may need to ask quiet questions to get some of the information. After fifteen minutes, have the teams stop looking. Have volunteers take turns reading their lists aloud.

Blending Words With *r*

Make a chart like the one below, leaving space for beginning consonants, blends, and digraphs before each ending. Then write blends, digraphs, and consonants on letter cards. Have children take turns making as many words with each ending as they can. You may want to post a list of words from the Word Bank on page 296 for children to use as a resource.

___ear	___ire	___irt	ch art
___ard	___are	___ore	___arm

Crossword Fun

Children can write simple two-word crossword puzzles using words with *r*-controlled vowels, and then exchange them with partners. For example:

Across:	not a boy
Down:	it goes on a car

Instant Activities

Who's Together? Give each child in the classroom an index card with an *r*-controlled vowel word. When you say "Start," have children look for other children whose words have the same vowel sound.

Line Up to Rhyme As children stand in line, say a word and have each child in the line, in turn, say a rhyming word. Use words like these: *car, store, bark, chair, part, arm, dirt, fire*. Accept rhyming words that have other vowel spellings.

Concentrate, Now! Use the Word and Picture Cards from pages 294–295 to play Concentration. (Tailor the number of cards to ability level.) Lay all the cards face down and have children take turns turning over two cards, attempting to match picture and word. If they do, they keep the cards. The one with the most cards at the end of the game wins.

Make Puzzles Invite children to write and illustrate a word with an *r*-controlled vowel. Then have them cut the card in half to make two puzzle pieces. Put children's puzzle pieces together in a pile and have volunteers take turns putting them back together.

Search for Vowel + r Invite children to take two minutes and look at a page in a story or reading book. Have them find as many words with *r*-controlled vowels as they can and list them on the chalkboard.

Add an r Write words like these on the chalkboard and invite children to make new words by inserting an *r* into each of them: *pat (part), cat (cart), ban (barn), tie (tire), skit (skirt), fist (first), chip (chirp), toe (tore), shot (short), cod (cord), spot (sport), bun (burn), cub (curb), fist (first)*. Have children say the words and listen for the way the vowel sound changes each time.

Riddle Me Invite children to choose a word with an *r*-controlled vowel and create a riddle for it. They should think of three clues that get easier. For example: "It is far away. It is up in the sky. You can see it at night." (a star) Have children present their riddles to the class, giving one clue at a time.

"Word Slide" Patterns

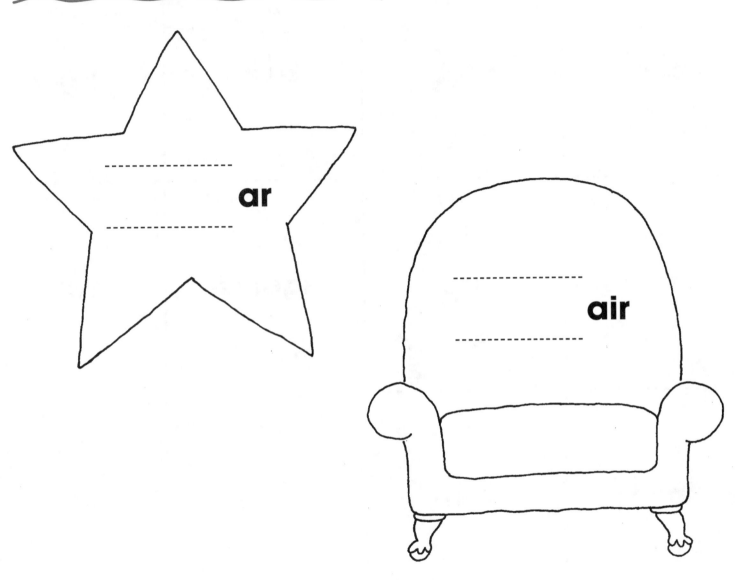

ar

air

strip 2   f   h   p   ch   st

strip 1   b   c   f   j   t   sc   st

Word Cards

car	star	barn	park
chair	tire	square	fern
shirt	oar	core	corn
nurse	fork	girl	horn

Picture Cards

Word Bank

Below is a list of words that you may use to illustrate words with *r*-controlled vowels. Some of these words are included in the Word/Picture Card set on pages 294–294. Ideas for using these cards and additional cards you may create yourself can be found in "Classroom Fun," pages 289–291.

Vowels With *r*

air	**are**	**ear**	**ore**	**ur**
chair	beware	clear	before	burn
fair	care	gear	chore	burst
hair	dare	hear	score	curb
pair	fare	rear	shore	curl
stair(s)	share	spear	snore	fur
	spare	tear	tore	surf
ar	stare	year	wore	turn
arm				
bark	**er**	**ire**	**or**	
charm	clerk	fire	acorn	
chart	fern	sire	corn	
farm	her	tire	form	
harm	herd	wire	forty	
jar	perch		horn	
scar	serve	**ir**	morning	
sharp	term	chirp	porch	
start		circus	short	
tar		first	thorn	
yarn		shirt	torch	
		skirt		
		third		
		thirty		
		twirl		

Teacher Notes

Page 272 See page 270, "Working with the Poem."

Page 273 *Answers:* jar, barn, car, cards, cart; *Riddle answer:* a car.

Page 274 *Answers:* Children will connect the stars in this order: arm, far, sharp, farm, dark, bark, star, smart, cart, tar, card, (and back up to arm); *Picture:* shark.

Page 275 *Answers:* shirt, girl, skirt, dirt, first, thirty.

Page 276 *Answers:* 1. a smart bird 2. a shark that parks 3. a dirty star 4. a car garden.

Page 277 *Answers:* Across: 2. fur 4. nurse 5. burn; Down: 1. purse 3. purr.

Page 278 *Answers:* clerk, serve; fern; her; perfect.

Page 279 *Game Directions:* Have pairs of children cut out the 15 word cards at the righthand side of the page, turn them face down, and mix them. Have each player take turns rolling a number cube and moving a marker that number of spaces. The player follows the directions in the space he or she lands on. If directions involve reading and/or using a word, the player draws a word card to use. The first player to reach home plate again wins.

Page 280 *Answers:* 1. chair 2. pair 3. stair 4. hair 5. fair.

Page 281 *Answers:* 1. year 2. ear 3. Dear 4. gear 5. tear.

Page 282 *Answers:* share, fare, care, dare, square, mare, spare, hare, scare, square.

Page 283 *Answers:* 1. tire 2. wire 3. score 4. store 5. shore.

Page 284 *Answers:* Children will color the square, horse, core, chair, stairs, fire, and tire; *Riddle answer:* stairs.

Page 285 *Answers:* Children will circle and write these words: square, chair, shark, hair, hear, bird, turn.

Page 286 *Answers:* 1. car 2. hair 3. purse 4. skirt 5. bird 6. gear 7. jar 8. tire 9. stork 10. care.

Phonograms With Short Vowels

Using This Book

Classroom Management

Reproducibles Reproducible pages 301–313 offer a variety of individual and partner activities. Answers or Game Directions appear as necessary in the *Teacher Notes* section on page 324.

Directions You may wish to go over the directions with children and verify that they can identify all picture cues before they begin independent work.

Games When children play partner games, circulate to make sure children understand procedures.

Working with the Poem

A poem on page 300 introduces the phonics element in this book, phonograms with short vowels. Start by reading the poem aloud to children. Duplicate the poem so children can work with it in a variety of ways:

Personal Response Read the poem aloud. Ask children if they think the poem is funny. Have children discuss tricks their own pets can do.

Phonemic Awareness You may wish to read the poem aloud and have children listen for a particular phonogram. For example, say, "Raise your hand when you hear a word that rhymes with *cup*."

Sound to Letter Write the poem on chart paper or on the chalkboard and have children point to words that rhyme. Then have them spell the letters that are the same in each rhyming word.

Connecting School and Home

The Family Letter on page 299 can be sent home to encourage families to reinforce what children are learning. Children will also enjoy sharing the Take-Home Book on pages 315–316. You can cut and fold these booklets ahead of time, or invite children to participate in the process. You might mount the pages on heavier stock so that you can place the Take-Home Book in your classroom library.

Word/Picture Card Sets

Pages 322–323 of this book contain matching sets of Word Cards and Picture Cards drawn from the vocabulary presented in this book. You may wish to mount these on heavier stock as a classroom resource. You may also wish to duplicate and distribute them to children for use in matching and sorting activities. Each child can use a large envelope to store the cards.

Assessment

Page 314, Show What You Know, provides children with targeted practice in standardized test-taking skills, using the content presented in this book in the assessment items.

Dear Family,

Your child is learning in school about phonograms with short vowels.

Phonograms are groups of ending letters that rhyme and are spelled the same. Some short vowel phonograms are *-an* in *fan* and *man*, and *-et* in *jet* and *net*.

bug   **rug**   **mug**

You may enjoy sharing some or all of the following activities with your child:

Make New Words

You can use any surface for writing — paper, a small chalkboard, or even a tray of sand — to practice making new words with phonograms. Write a word like *cat* and erase the *c*. Have your child write another consonant letter to make a new word. Check to be sure the new word is real, not a nonsense word.

Say a Rhyme

When you see a short vowel word in environmental print (at the grocery store, or on a road sign), ask your child to name a word or two that rhymes with it. (For example: *stop, shop, cop, hop*)

Reading Together

To practice reading words with short vowel phonograms, look over your child's Take-Home Book, "What Is It?" Ask your child to find words with short vowel phonograms, read each word to you, and think of a rhyming word. You may also wish to look for these books in your local library:

Sincerely,

In My Backyard
by John DeVries

Duckat
by Gaelyn Gordon

Name _____

Spot's Trick

Mom! Dad!
Run here quick!
Spot can do
A brand new trick!
If you set a cup
Next to the pup,
He knocks it over
Then picks it up!

Phonograms With Short Vowels

The Great Big Book of Fun Phonics Activities © Scholastic Professional Books

Name _____

Rhyming Puzzles

Find two pictures whose names rhyme. Write the missing letters. Cut out the puzzle piece. Paste it where it fits.

1.
cab

2.
Dad

3.
cat

4.
van

5.
lap

f ___ ___

m ___ ___

s ___ ___

h ___ ___

c r ___ ___

Name _____

Frog Prince

Color the Frog Prince. Use the colors in the color key. Then answer the question. Use a word you have colored.

Rhymes with cob = blue
Rhymes with pot = red
Rhymes with frog = yellow
Rhymes with mop = green

Where does a Frog Prince sit? On the top _____og.

The Great Big Book of Fun Phonics Activities © Scholastic Professional Books

Name _____

Word Steps

Complete the word steps. Write a letter to end a word. Then use the same letter to begin the next word. You will use each word in the box once. The first set is done for you.

| bat | job | map | nap | not | top |
| pan | pop | ran | hot | pad | tap |

1.

h o <u>t</u>

<u>t</u> o <u>p</u>

<u>p</u> a d

2.

m a ___

___ a ___

___ o t

3.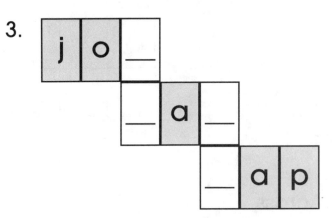

j o ___

___ a ___

___ a p

4.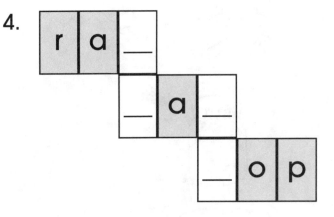

r a ___

___ a ___

___ o p

Name _____

Crossword Puzzle

Read the words in the box. Look at the picture clues.
Write each word in the puzzle.

| lid | pig | dig | ship | swim |

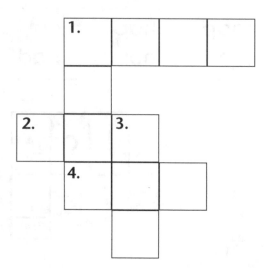

Across

1.

2.

4.

Down

1.

3.

Short **i** Phonograms **-id, -ig, -im, -ip**

The Great Big Book of Fun Phonics Activities © Scholastic Professional Books

Picture This

Read the sentences. Write the letters to finish each picture label. Then draw the picture.

1. This is a pet.

   This is a vet.

a p___ ___ at the v___ ___

2. This is a ten.

   These are men.

t___ ___ m___ ___

3. This is baby Ted.

   This is his bed.

T___ ___ in his b___ ___

4. This is a hen.

   This is a pen.

a h___ ___ in her p___ ___

Read and Rhyme

Say the word next to each number. Look at the pictures whose names rhyme with it. Add a letter to finish each rhyming name. You will use each letter in the box once.

b	c	h	j	m	n	r	s

1. but

___ ut

___ ut

3. fun

___ un

___ un

2. rug

___ ug

___ ug

4. tug

___ ug

___ ug

Animal Match

Cut out all the words with a partner. Then play Animal Match. Your teacher will tell you how to play.

Player 1

Player 2

cat	cat	cat
pig	pig	pig
hen	hen	hen
bug	bug	bug
rat	rat	rat
crab	crab	crab
bat	bat	bat
frog	frog	frog

Name _____

Down the Stairs

Help Bill and Nick climb down from the top floor.
Follow the words that rhyme with their names.

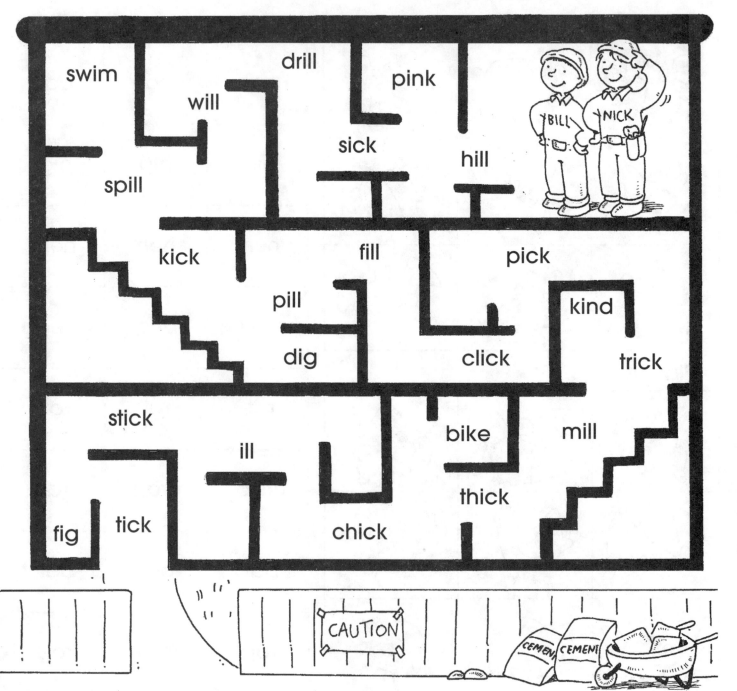

swim
will
drill
pink
sick
hill
spill
kick
fill
pick
pill
dig
click
kind
trick
stick
bike
mill
ill
thick
fig
tick
chick

CAUTION
CEMENT CEMENT

Short i Phonograms -ick, -ill

Name _____

Happy Endings

Look at each picture and its name. Then find a picture and name that rhyme with them at the bottom of the page. Cut and paste them in the boxes. You will not use all the pictures or names.

Picture	Name	Picture	Name
1.	duck		
2.	sock		
3.	jack		

	clock		truck
chick		crack	

Name _____

Be a Poet!

Circle the rhyming words in each box. Then write the words where they belong to finish each poem.

1. | mop   dock   clock   rope   tock   rock |

There once was a _____,

That fell off the _____.

It hit a _____.

Splash!

No more tick-_____!

2. | lock   flock   window   knock   mother   shock |

I heard a _____,

So I opened the _____.

What a _____!

There was a lost sheep

Looking for its _____.

Name _____

The King's Things

Look at each picture. Read the two words below it. Color the word that tells about the picture. Then tell the story.

drink   think

sink   string

Sing   sting

ink   mink

ring   pink

The Great Big Book of Fun Phonics Activities © Scholastic Professional Books

Rhyme and Sort

These words are all mixed up!
Write the words that rhyme with **bank** in the bank.
Write the words that rhyme with **trunk** in the trunk.

junk	blank	sank	tank
skunk	thank	clunk	bunk

Short Vowel Phonograms **-ank, -unk**

The Great Big Book of Fun Phonics Activities © Scholastic Professional Books

Name _____

Sink or Swim

You can be the frog, the pig, the bug, or the skunk.
You must swim to the riverbank. Your teacher will tell
you how to play the game.

Riverbank

Markers

Number Cards

Name _____

Show What You Know

Read the word in each row. Fill in the circle next to the pictures whose names rhyme with the word.

1. fat ○ ○ ○

2. hop ○ ○ ○

3. fun ○ ○ ○

4. rug ○ ○ ○

5. dock ○ ○ ○

6. tan ○ ○ ○

7. get ○ ○

8. luck ○ ○ ○

9. hut ○ ○ ○

10. wing ○ ○

The Great Big Book of Fun Phonics Activities © Scholastic Professional Books

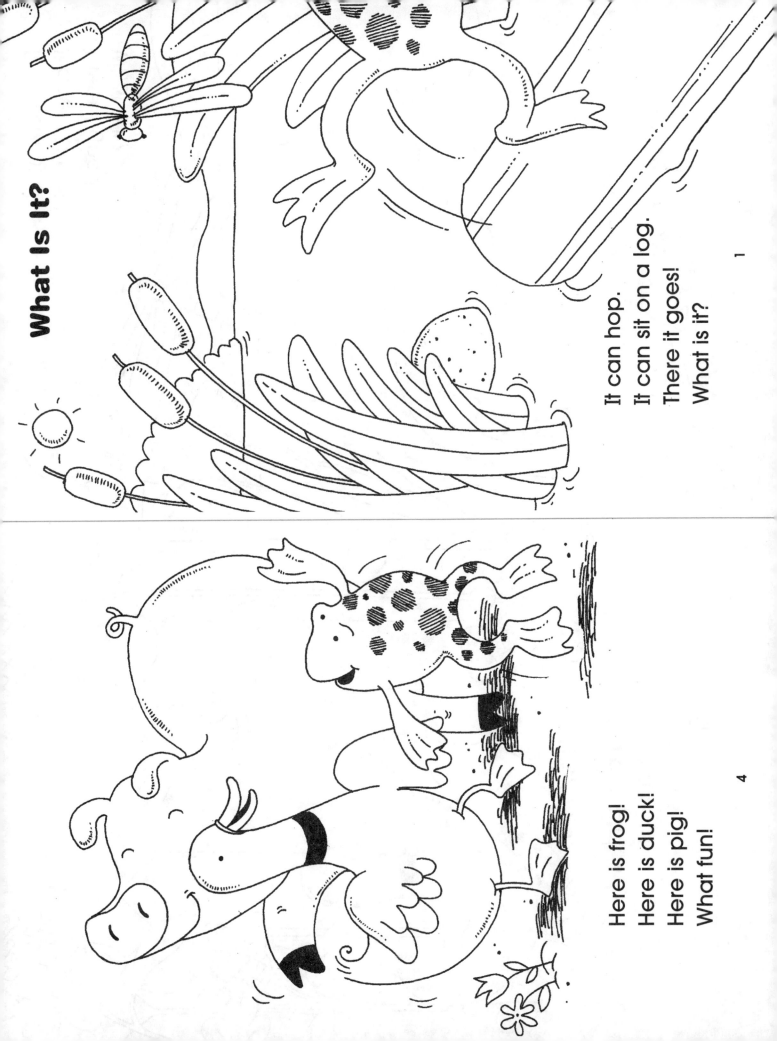

What Is It?

It can hop.
It can sit on a log.
There it goes!
What is it?

1

Here is frog!
Here is duck!
Here is pig!
What fun!

4

It can swim.
It goes "Quack!"
There it goes!
What is it?

2

It is big and pink.
It lives in a pen.
There it goes!
What is it?

3

Classroom Fun

Phonograms with Short Vowels

Rhyming Fun

Ask children to brainstorm words with short vowel phonograms that rhyme. List their suggestions on the chalkboard. You may also list words from the Word Bank on page 324. Then invite children to choose two words that rhyme and write or dictate a phrase that uses the two words. Suggest models such as *a wet pet* or *a sick chick* and encourage children to be silly and creative in their thinking. Have them illustrate their phrases to display in the class.

a sick chick

Crossword Fun

Challenge children to think of two words that rhyme and create a simple puzzle for a classmate to solve. For example:

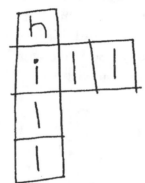

Across: it means "sick."
Down: Jack and Jill went up this.

Create a Poem

Children can write guided poems. Write a frame like the one below on chart paper and work together with small groups to fill in the blanks:

> There once was a big black cat,
> Who wore a big black _____. (hat)
> He slept on a fuzzy pink _____. (mat)
> What do you think about _____? (that)

Encourage children's creativity, and lead them to try out other substitutions with words that rhyme with *hen, frog, skunk, pig,* and *duck.* Invite children to illustrate their poems.

Classroom Fun

Word Slide

Make a word slide for the phonogram *-at*. Cut out a cat shape and run a letter strip through slits so children can make new words, such as *bat, cat, fat, hat, mat, vat, rat, sat, pat, flat, that, chat.* You may wish to use the word slide with individuals or in a small group. As children pronounce each new rhyming word, have them use it in a sentence. You may also make word slides for other phonograms you wish to practice.

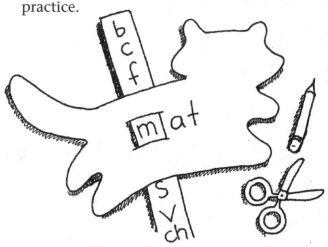

Phonogram Footprints

Write words that feature two or three phonograms on cutouts of large footprints, one word to a footprint. Lay them out in a path and have children walk along the path, saying each word aloud as they go. You can also have them walk only on the footprints that have words with a certain phonogram.

Word-Part Cards

Using index cards or tagboard, make cards for short vowel phonograms, beginning consonants, consonant digraphs, and consonant blends. Then let children take turns making new words with each phonogram by substituting different beginning sounds. As they make each new word, invite them to use it in a sentence. You may also want to display the word-part cards, call out words, and have children find the letters that make the new word. For example, you could say, "Make *thick*, now *chick*, now *pick*."

Word Ladders

Invite children to make word ladders with rhyming words, substituting the initial consonant sound to make a new word. Let them work with partners at the chalkboard and create as many rhyming words as they can. Assign each pair a different phonogram. Have partners underline the part of the word that has changed.

and
band
hand
land
sand
stand

Dick
Kick
Pick
Sick
Stick
click

Short Vowel Phonogram Big Book

Invite small groups of children to work together to create a short vowel pictionary big book. Assign each group a phonogram and have them brainstorm a list of words with that phonogram. Then, have each child choose one word to illustrate and label on a large piece of construction paper. Bind each group's contribution into a class big book. At the end of the day, let each group read its dictionary entries aloud.

Rhyming Concentration

Use the Word Cards and/or the Picture Cards on pages 323–325 with small groups of children to play the game Rhyming Concentration. Place the cards face down on a table in neat rows. Then have children take turns turning up two cards at a time, attempting to match words that rhyme or matching words and pictures. If the two cards match, the child keeps the pair and takes another turn. If the two cards do not match, the next child takes a turn. When all the cards have been taken, the game is over. The child with the most cards wins.

Phonogram Word Wheel

Using the Phonogram Wheel Pattern on page 321, cut out two circles and mount them on cardboard. Use a paper fastener to fasten them together in the center. Make sure the wheels turn easily. The outer circle should have beginning consonants and clusters, and the inner circle should have phonograms which align with them. Invite children to turn the wheel until they can read a word. Then have them say and write other words that rhyme with it. You can make your own custom phonogram wheels to help children practice troublesome phonograms.

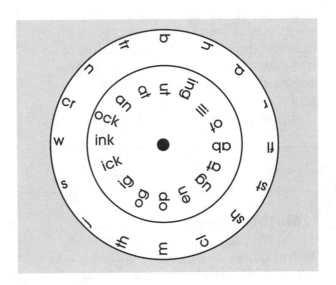

Instant Activities

Pop Up! Ask children to pop up (stand) when they hear a word that rhymes with *pop*. Say words like *cop, Bob, mop, bug, hop, got, flop, top, crop, duck, stick, drop, shop, ship, stop.*

Quick Sort Children can sort the Word and Picture Cards from pages 322–323 by phonograms and short vowel sound (all short *a* sounds, for example). Encourage them to find class-room items to add to each grouping.

Sand or Chalk Game Write a short vowel word in a sand tray or on the chalkboard. Then ask a volunteer to make a new word by erasing the beginning consonant sound and replacing it with another letter. Give children plenty of thinking time.

Mother, May I? Have children stand in a straight line and play the Mother, May I? game. Let children take one step forward only if they hear a pair of words that rhyme. Say pairs like *plan/tan, drop/drip, swing/king, sock/lock, blank/sank, black/green, lot/not, spill/spin, lip/sip.*

Where's the Envelope? Make envelopes for short *a* phonograms (*-ab, -ack, -ad -an, -ank, -at*). Have children sort the Picture Cards and other pictures they have collected into the appropriate envelopes. Repeat for each short vowel sound and its phonograms.

A Hat for a Day Draw the outline of a hat on chart paper and write *hat*. Then, during the day have children take turns writing words that rhyme with *hat*. Each day, focus on a different phonogram with a different picture. (For example: a trunk for *-unk*, a jet for *-et*.)

Mystery Cards Have volunteers choose a Picture Card and keep it hidden. Have them describe the picture without naming it. When the class guesses the picture name, have children suggest a word that rhymes with it.

Say "Quack!" Ask children to imagine they are ducks and to quack each time you say a word that rhymes with *quack*. Say words like: *sack, back, at, black, blue, crack, snack, track, trick, jack.*

Phonogram Wheel Pattern

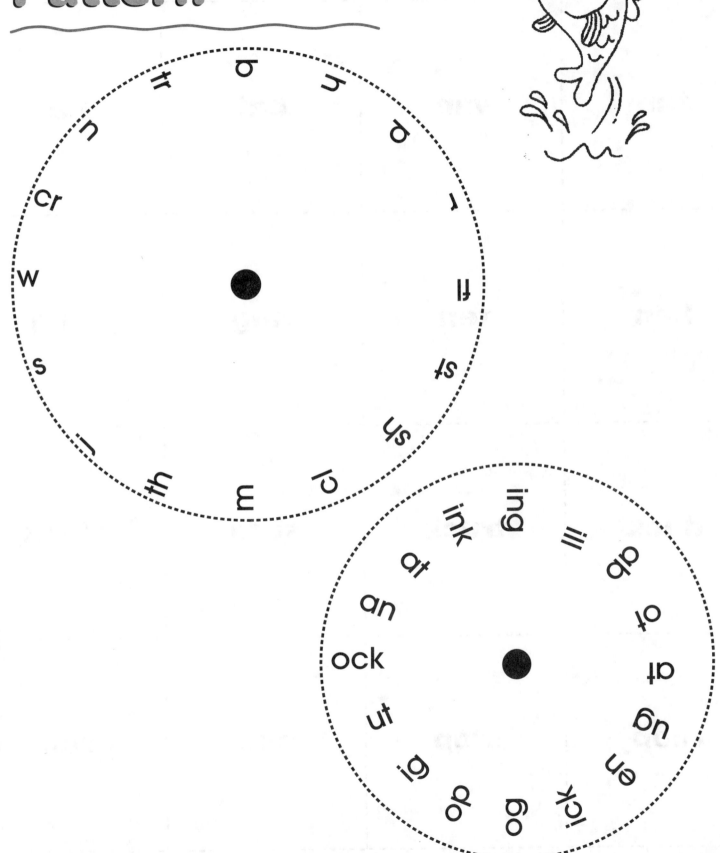

Word Cards

fan	van	bat	hat
hen	ten	ring	king
duck	truck	sock	clock
mop	stop	sun	run

Picture Cards

Word Bank

Below is a list of words that you may use to illustrate phonograms with short vowels. Some of these words are included in the Word/Picture Card set on pages 322–323. Ideas for using these cards and additional cards you may create yourself can be found in "Classroom Fun," pages 317–319.

Phonograms With Short Vowels

ab	**at**	**ig**	**ing**	**un**
cab	mat	big	spring	bun
crab	sat	dig	swing	fun
ack	that	**im**	thing	run
quack	**ed**	him	**ock**	**ut**
snack	fed	swim	clock	but
ad	red	**ip**	sock	hut
glad	sled	sip	**og**	shut
had	**en**	slip	frog	**ug**
mad	den	trip	log	bug
an	pen	**ill**	**ob**	hug
plan	when	drill	cob	rug
than	**et**	spill	job	**uck**
ank	get	**ick**	**op**	duck
blank	wet	sick	drop	luck
sank	yet	thick	hop	truck
thank	**id**	**ink**	top	**unk**
ap	hid	pink	**ot**	junk
clap	kid	think	got	skunk
lap	slid	wink	hot	trunk
tap				

Teacher Notes

Page 300 See page 298, "Working with the Poem."

Page 301 *Answers:* 1. cab—crab 2. Dad—sad 3. cat—hat 4. van—fan 5. lap—map.

Page 302 *Answers:* blue: job, knob, rob, sob; red: spot, hot, not, got; yellow: dog, jog, bog, log, fog; green: top, hop, pop, shop, stop; *Riddle Answer:* top log.

Page 303 *Answers:* 1. hot, top, pad 2. map, pan, not 3. job, bat, tap 4. ran, nap, pop.

Page 304 *Answers:* Across—1. swim 2. lid 4. pig; Down—1. ship 3. dig.

Page 305 *Answers:* 1. Children draw a pet and the vet and complete *pet, vet*; 2. Children draw ten men and complete *ten, men*; 3. Children draw Ted in his bed and complete *Ted, bed*; 4. Children draw a hen in her pen and complete *hen, pen*.

Page 306 *Answers:* 1. nut, cut 2. bug, jug 3. run, sun 4. hug, mug.

Page 307 *Game Directions:* Each child uses one gameboard. Children take turns drawing a word and placing it over the matching picture. If they have already covered that picture, they lose the turn. FREE is a free space. The first child to cover all eight other spaces wins. Children can switch gameboards and play again.

Page 308 *Answers:* hill, sick, drill, will, spill, kick, pill, fill, click, pick, trick, mill, thick, chick, ill, stick, tick.

Page 309 *Answers:* 1. picture of truck, word *truck* 2. picture of clock, word *clock* 3. picture of cup with crack, word *crack*.

Page 310 *Answers:* 1. clock, dock, rock, tock. 2. knock, lock, shock, flock.

Page 311 *Answers:* 1. king 2. sing 3. think 4. ink 5. sink 6. ring.

Page 312 *Answers:* Inside bank: blank, sank, thank, tank. Inside trunk: junk, clunk, skunk, bunk.

Page 313 *Game Directions:* Children cut out markers and each choose one to place on the Start arrow. They cut out number cards and turn the number cards over. Children take turns choosing one and moving a marker that many spaces, saying the word in the space they land on. If they can say a rhyming word, they can stay there. If not, they go back to the previous position and play passes to the next child. The first one to reach the riverbank wins.

Page 314 *Answers:* 1. cat, bat 2. mop, stop 3. sun, run 4. hug, mug 5. lock, clock 6. pan, van 7. net, jet 8. duck, truck 9. cut, nut 10. king, ring.

Phonograms With Long Vowels

Using This Book

Classroom Management

Reproducibles Reproducible pages 329–341 offer a variety of individual and partner activities. Simple directions to the children are augmented when necessary by *Answers* or *Game Directions* in the *Teacher Notes* Section on page 352.

Directions You may wish to go over the directions with children and verify that they can identify all picture cues before they begin independent work.

Games When children play partner games, you may want to circulate in order to make sure that children understand procedures.

Working with the Poem

A poem on page 328 introduces the phonics element in this book, phonograms with long vowels. Start by reading this page aloud to children. As children progress through the activities in this book, you may want to duplicate the poem so children can work with it in a variety of ways:

Personal Response Read the poem aloud and have students talk about it. Ask if they enjoy the activities described in the poem.

Phonemic Awareness Read the poem aloud. Ask children to raise their hands when they hear long vowel sounds.

Sound to Letter Write the poem on a chart, and ask children to point to or circle words that begin or end with long vowel phonograms.

Innovation Ask children to brainstorm ideas first. Then duplicate one line or more of the poem, leaving a blank. Encourage children to "write" an original verse by filling in the blank.

Connecting School and Home

The Family Letter on page 327 can be sent home to encourage families to reinforce what children are learning. Children will also enjoy sharing the Take-Home Book on pages 343–344. You can cut and fold these booklets ahead of time, or invite children to participate in the process. You may also mount the pages on heavier stock so you can place the Take-Home Book in your classroom library.

Word/Picture Card Sets

Pages 350–351 of this book contain matching sets of Word/Picture Cards drawn from the vocabulary presented in this book. You may wish to mount these on heavier stock as a classroom resource. You may also wish to duplicate and distribute them to children for use in matching and sorting activities. Each child can use a large envelope to store the cards.

Assessment

Page 342, Show What You Know, provides children with targeted practice in standardized test-taking skills, using the content presented in this book in the assessment items.

Dear Family,

In school, your child is learning about phonograms with long vowels. Phonograms are groups of ending letters that rhyme and are spelled the same. Some long vowel phonograms are *-ame* in n*ame* and g*ame*, *-old* in g*old* and h*old*.

c**one**

ph**one**

You may enjoy sharing some or all of the following activities with your child:

Rhyming Sentences

With your child, brainstorm a list of words that rhyme and have long vowel sounds (for example: *knight, fight, night, light*). Then ask your child to make up a little story using these words and tell it to other family members.

Riddles

Choose one of the words your child listed and ask him or her to make up a riddle for it. For example: *It is something we eat on. It ends with -ate. (plate)*

Reading Together

To practice reading words with long vowel phonograms, look over your child's Take-Home Book, "Hide and Seek!" Ask your child to point to long vowel phonograms and to try to think of a rhyming word for each one. You may also wish to look for these books in your local library:

Sincerely,

Bringing the Rain to Kapiti Plain
by Verna Aardema

Miss Nelson Has a Field Day
by Harry Allard

Name _____

Nice Day

Nice day!
Time to play!
Skate and bike!
Take a hike!
Climb the trees!
Race the breeze!
Wait! Bad news!
Holes in my shoes!

Name _____

Rhyming Riddles

Read each riddle. Write the answer. Use words from the box. Then cut and paste the picture that shows each answer.

| face | skate | gate | lake | race |

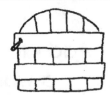

1. I keep things out.
   I keep things in.
   I rhyme with **date**.

   I am a _____.

2. I have eyes. I have a mouth.
   I rhyme with **place**.

   I am your _____.

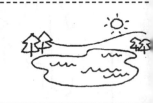

3. You can put me on.
   I rhyme with **late**.

   I am a _____.

4. You can run in me.
   I rhyme with **lace**.

   I am a _____.

5. You can swim in me.
   I rhyme with **snake**.

   I am a _____.

Name _____

Magic Tricks

Follow the magician's directions. Write each new word in the magic box. Use words from the word box. Cut and paste the matching picture above each word.

| rain | snail | train | trail | pail |

Add r to make a word.

_____ ain

1. Now, add t.

_____

2. Now, change the n to l.

_____

3. Now, change the tr to p.

_____

4. Now, change the p to sn.

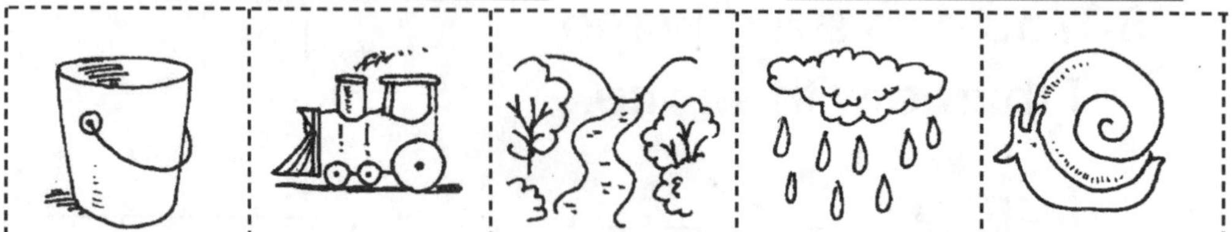

_____

Long **a** Phonograms **ail, ain**

The Great Big Book of Fun Phonics Activities © Scholastic Professional Books

Name _____

Mini Crosswords

Look at the mini crossword puzzles next to each number. Write **a** in the middle space to make two words. Write the two words on the lines.

1.

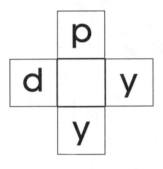

_____

_____

2.

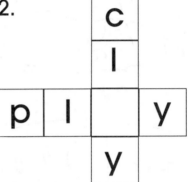

_____

_____

3.

_____

_____

4.

_____

_____

Name _____

Rhyme and Go

Do a spin.
Take an
extra turn.

What
rhymes
with
face?

START

Fall down.
Go back 1
space.

What is
a tale?

Thin ice.
Go back up.

FINISH

Long **a** Phonograms

The Great Big Book of Fun Phonics Activities © Scholastic Professional Books

Name _____

Sleep Tight!

Color the sheep with **eep** words red.
Color the sheep with **eet** words green.
Color the sheep with **eed** words yellow.
Then find all the words in the puzzle. Circle them.
They can go down or across.

E	E	S	W	F	E	E
S	T	R	E	E	T	H
E	E	B	E	E	T	R
E	E	A	D	T	J	E
D	L	E	E	D	E	E
S	N	E	W	P	E	T
E	S	L	E	E	P	E

Name _____

Flip for Riddles

Help Neal do some flips. Look at the riddles on the gym mat. Match each one to a word from the word box. Write each word.

seat	real	steam
treat	seal	team

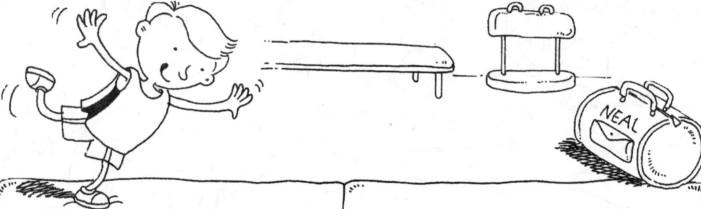

1. I have nine players.
   We try to win!

   _____

2. I am something you like to eat.

   _____

3. I am hot.
   I make a hissing noise.

   _____

4. I am an animal. I can balance a ball on my nose.

   _____

5. I am not make-believe.

   _____

6. I am on the bus.
   You sit on me.

   _____

The Great Big Book of Fun Phonics Activities © Scholastic Professional Books

Name _____

Drop a Coin

Drop a coin. Write a rhyme.
Your teacher will tell you what to do.

-ain	-eal	-eam
_____	_____	_____
-ay	-eat	-ake
_____	_____	_____
-eep	-ail	-eed
_____	_____	_____
-ace	-ean	-ate
_____	_____	_____

place	real	rain	clean	mail	sweep
state	take	steam	stay	seat	seed

The Great Big Book of Fun Phonics Activities © Scholastic Professional Books

Name _____

Nice Rhymes

Look at each picture. Say the picture name. Then read the words in the center of the page. Draw a line from each word to the picture that rhymes with it.

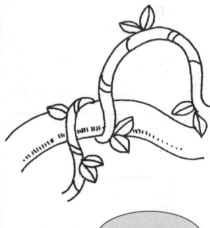

(hide)

(mine)

(nice)

Now write the word that has the most rhymes. _____

Name _____

Fight the Dragon

Help the knight find the dragon. Follow the long **i** words
in the maze. Then write **ight** to finish each sentence below.

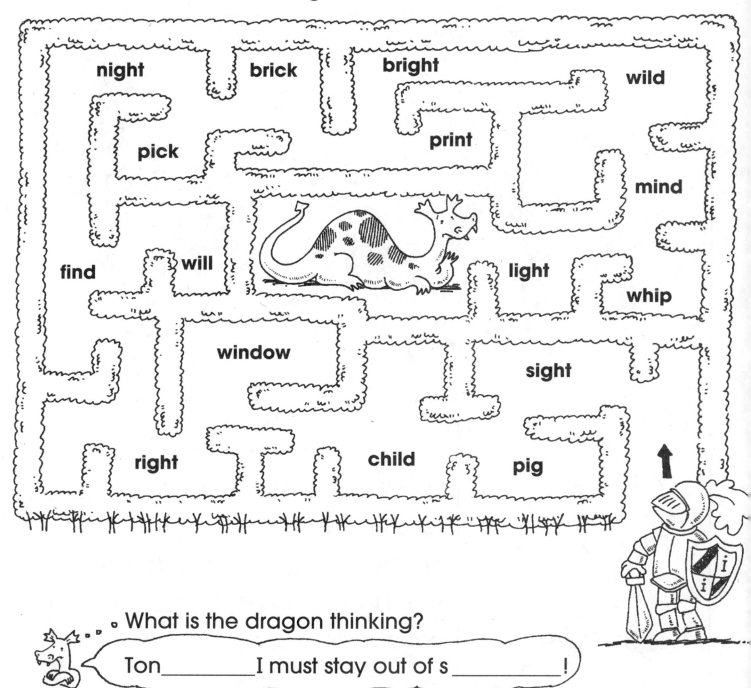

night   brick   bright   wild

print

pick

mind

find   will   light   whip

window   sight

right   child   pig

What is the dragon thinking?

Ton_____ I must stay out of s _____!

Name _____

My Report

Look at the scene. Then finish Ty's report. Use words from the box.

| fly | sky | try | cry | shy |

My Report
by Ty

I like the park. I look up in the _____.

I see two things that _____. I see a

girl. She will _____ to ride a bike. I

see a boy. He looks _____. I see a

baby. "Don't _____, baby."

The End

Name _____

Rhyming Puzzles

Find two pictures whose names rhyme. Write the rhyming word. Cut out the puzzle piece. Paste it where it fits. Match up all the rhyming puzzles.

1.
tow

2.
cone

3.
phone

4.
cold

5.
old

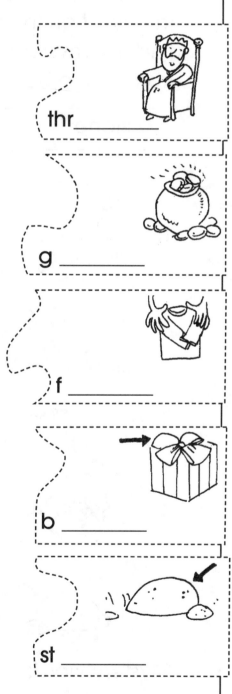

thr_____

g _____

f _____

b _____

st _____

Name _____

Mystery Word

What keeps monsters away at night?

Find the name of each picture in the word box. Write the word on the lines. Put one letter on each line. Now find the mystery word. Read the letters in the tall box from top to bottom. Write the mystery word.

stone	knight	mice	slide	night

1.    1. ____ ____ ____ ____ ____

2.    2. ____ ____ ____ ____

3.    3. ____ ____ ____ ____ ____

4.  4. ____ ____ ____ ____ ____ ____

5.    5. ____ ____ ____ ____ ____

Mystery word: _____ .

Long **o** and Long **i** Phonograms

Name _____

Crossword Fun

Read the words in the box. Look at the picture clues.
Write each word in the puzzle.

skate	phone	knight
game	mice	sheep

Across

2.

3.

5.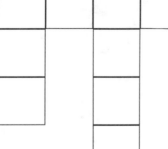

Down

1.

4.

6.

Name _____

Show What You Know

Read the word in each row. Fill in the circle next to the picture that rhymes with the word.

1. sky   ○    ○   ○

2. make   ○    ○   ○

3. place   ○    ○   ○

4. fold   ○    ○   ○

5. brain   ○   ○    ○

6. fail   ○    ○    ○

7. keep   ○   ○    ○

8. greet   ○    ○   ○

9. light   ○   ○   ○

10. line   ○   ○   ○

Hide and Seek

Everybody's hiding.
Where can they be?
I'm going to find them.
Who will I see?

It's Twinkletoes!

I see you, Jane, up on the slide.
I see you, Ray, you can't hide.
I spy you, Kate, behind that tree.
And, Jake, is that really you I see?

2

And who is that?
I see your nose.
Help me guess...

3

Classroom Fun •••••

Phonograms with Long Vowels

Phonogram, Phonogram, Goose!

Play a version of Duck, Duck, Goose. First, say a word with a long vowel phonogram and have children brainstorm a list of words that rhyme with the word. Appoint one child to be "It," and have the other children squat in a circle. Then have "It" walk around the circle, touching each child's shoulder and saying a rhyming word each time. When "It" cannot think of another rhyming word, he or she yells "Goose!" and taps the next child. The "Goose" chases "It" around the circle. If "It" gets back to the "Goose's" spot before being tagged, he or she is safe and the "Goose" is then "It." If not, "It" tries again with another word.

Word Ladders

Begin a word ladder, and invite children to substitute one beginning or ending consonant sound in each "step" to make a new word. You may wish to let children substitute long vowel sounds as well. Have children underline the part of the word that has been changed.

date	face
late	race
lake	rice
take	mice
shake	mine
shame	mane
name	make
fame	wake

Telling Stories

On chart paper write the following silly story titles or others you invent. Invite volunteers to choose one title and make up an oral story about it:

- The Night the Knight Got in a Fight
- Two Nice Mice
- A Train with a Brain
- The Snail Who Needed a Nail

Either record children's stories on an audio cassette recorder or have children dictate them to you. Encourage each child to draw a picture about his or her story when it is finished and label it with the title. Display children's story illustrations on a bulletin board.

Classroom Fun

Hang It Up!

Hang a string across the classroom like a clothesline. Provide a box holding clothes pins and either cards or construction-paper scraps. At one end of the string, hang up a word with a long vowel phonogram, such as *cane*. During the day, have children hang up as many other words with that phonogram as they can. When all *-ane* words have been exhausted, ask children to suggest a word with another phonogram.

Human Phonograms

Give each child in the classroom these letters written on large cards: *a, e, i, o, c, k, l, m, n, t, y, d, p, s, b, r, f, g, h,* and *w.* Explain that when you say a word with a long vowel phonogram, the children holding letters that spell the word should come forward. Then, have the children forming the phonogram ask classmates who have letters that make blends, digraphs or single consonant sounds to come forward to make new words with the phonogram. When all combinations have been exhausted with a phonogram, start with a new one.

Phonogram Frames

Let pairs or small groups of children use the Phonogram Frames on page 349 to play a game. Have each child work with one frame. Cut out the word beginnings (consonant blends, consonant digraphs, and single consonants), and turn them face down. Have children take turns choosing a beginning sound and putting it in the frame to make a word. Then have the player either tell what the word means or use it in a sentence. If no combinations make a word or the child cannot think of a definition or sentence, have him or her put the beginning letter(s) face down again. The first child to fill his or her board with words wins.

ace	ail	r̲ake	ight
s̲h̲ ine	s̲ ay	ice	old

Key Ring Phonograms

You can use a key ring to help children practice making several words with the same phonogram. On a 1" x 3" card cut from tagboard or poster board, write a long vowel phonogram such as -ine. Punch a hole in the end of the card and put it on the key ring. Then cut out smaller cards measuring 1" x 2". On each of these, write a beginning consonant, a consonant blend, or a consonant digraph (for example, *f, p, l, m, d, sp, sh, wh*). Encourage children to flip the cards to make several words with the same phonogram.

Jumping Phonograms!

Draw a square with a design like the one below, either on the playground with chalk or on the classroom floor with masking tape. Have children play individually. Give the child designated as "the jumper" a handful of beans. As you call out a long vowel phonogram, have the child jump to that shape and put down a bean. When all the shapes have markers, let the next child play the game.

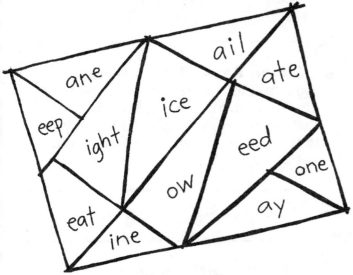

To make the game more challenging, you can have the child say as many rhyming words with each phonogram as he or she can. Have the child place one bean in the shape for each rhyming word. Count the beans after each child's turn. The child who places the most beans wins.

Find Your Team!

On index cards, write single words covering a number of different long vowel phonograms. For example:

-**old** (*gold, hold, told, mold, fold*)
-**ild** (*wild, child, mild*)
-**ind** (*find, mind, bind, behind, kind*)
-**ail** (*mail, tail, nail, pail , rail, sail*)
-**ate** (*ate, date, gate, late, slate*)
-**ice** (*nice, twice, mice, price, spice*)
-**eet** (*beet, feet, greet, meet, sheet*)

Distribute one word card to each child. Tell children that when you say "Go," they are to say their word aloud quietly as they walk around the room, listening for other players saying words that rhyme with theirs. When they find other players who have a word with the same phonogram, they are to stay together. At the end of a few minutes, see if all the members of each team have found one another.

Instant Activities

Beep Like a Jeep Ask children to beep like a jeep when they hear a word that rhymes with jeep. Say words like these: *beep, feed, jeep, cream, sheep, beet, keep, sleep, name, deep.*

Draw It! Let each child brainstorm a list of words for a long vowel phonogram. Then have the child draw a picture, including representations for as many words as he or she can. Encourage creativity. For example, for *-ide*, the child could draw a dog that is *hiding*, someone who is *riding*, a *wide* truck, and the *side* of an object.

Hold Up a Card Give out index cards, and have each child write one long *a* phonogram on his or her card (*-ace, -ake, -ame, -ane, -ate, -ain,* or *-ay*). Then, as you call out random words with long *a* phonograms, have children hold up their cards when they hear a word that has their phonogram.

Phonogram Mailboxes Use shoe boxes to make mailboxes for sorting words. Write a different phonogram on the outside of each shoe box and cut a slit in the top large enough to accept index cards. Write words with long vowel phonograms on cards, and have children sort them into the different mailboxes.

Simon Says Play Simon Says. Explain that children are to follow the direction only if they hear two words that rhyme. For example: "Simon says touch your toe when he says *brake* and *flake.*"

Color the Difference On the chalkboard, write a list of words that have the same phonogram, such as *feed, weed, seed,* and *speed.* Then have children take turns using colored chalk to circle the part of each word that is different.

Phonogram for a Day Draw the outline of a snake on chart paper. Invite children to come up during the day and write words on the snake that have the same phonogram as *snake.* Repeat the activity each day, focusing on a different long vowel phonogram and picture.

Phonogram Frames

ace	ail	ake	ight
ine	ay	ice	old

ain	eep	eed	ide
ild	ane	ame	one

wh	sn	tr	g	j	fr	r	n	bl	m
c	ch	st	s	w	f	n	b	sh	br

Word Cards

cake	snake	skate	plate
wheat	meat	jeep	sheep
bride	slide	mice	rice
knight	cold	gold	cry

Picture Cards

Word Bank

Below is a list of words that you may use to illustrate words with long vowel phonograms. Some of these words are included in the Word/Picture Card set on pages 350–351. Ideas for using these cards and additional cards you may create yourself can be found in "Classroom Fun," pages 345–347.

Phonograms With Long Vowels

ace	**ate**	**eam**	**ide**	**old**
lace	crate	cream	bride	bold
place	date	dream	hide	gold
race	gate	team	side	scold
ake	**ain**	**eed**	**ine**	**one**
bake	brain	feed	fine	bone
brake	chain	seed	nine	phone
make	rain	weed	shine	stone
ail	**ay**	**eep**	**ight**	**ow**
mail	day	deep	bright	blow
nail	hay	jeep	light	know
snail	play	sleep	night	show
ame	**eat**	**eet**	**ild**	**y**
came	eat	beet	child	dry
frame	meat	greet	mild	fly
game	seat	street	wild	shy
ane	**eal**	**ice**	**ind**	
cane	meal	mice	blind	
mane	real	price	find	
plane	seal	spice	mind	

Teacher Notes

Page 328 See page 326, "Working with the Poem."

Page 329 *Answers:* 1. gate 2. face 3. skate 4. race 5. lake.

Page 330 *Answers:* rain, 1. train, 2. trail, 3. pail, 4. snail.

Page 331 *Answers:* 1. pay, day 2. clay, play 3. mane, cane 4. crane, plane

Page 332 *Game Directions:* Have children take turns rolling a number cube and moving a marker that many spaces. Have them say the picture name in the space where they land and then say a rhyming word for it. If they do, they can stay there. If they cannot, they must return to the previous location. If they land on a space that has a short cut, they can take the short cut— but only if they answer the question.

Page 333 *Answers:* Red—sleep, jeep; Green—street, feet; Yellow —weed, seed. Children will circle all the words listed here in the puzzle.

Page 334 *Answers:* 1. team 2. treat 3. steam 4. seal 5. real 6. seat.

Page 335 *Directions:* Have children cut out all the words at the bottom of the page and sort them into two groups: those with long *a* phonograms and those with long *e* phonograms. Distribute coins or other small heavy markers. Tell children to drop the coin onto the page. The child must find a word that uses the same ending that's shown in the box where the coin has landed, and paste it in place. Then he or she must write a rhyming word with the same spelling on the line in the box. Invite children to share their rhyming words with the class. You may wish to have pairs of children collaborate on this page. Answers: Long *a* words: place, rain, mail, state, take, stay. Long *e* words: real, clean, sweep, steam, seat, seed.

Page 336 *Answers:* hide—slide, bride; mine—nine, vine; nice—mice, price, rice. Children will write the word *nice*.

Page 337 *Answers:* sight, child, right, find, night, bright, wild, mind, light. Children will write *ight* to finish the words *Tonight, sight.*

Page 338 *Answers:* sky, fly, try, shy, cry.

Page 339 *Answers:* 1. tow—bow 2. cone—throne 3. phone—stone 4. cold—gold 5. old—fold.

Page 340 *Answers:* 1. slide 2. mice 3. night 4. knight 5. stone. *Mystery word:* light.

Page 341 *Answers:* Across: 2. sheep 3. skate 5. game. Down: 1. phone 4. knight 6. mice.

Page 342 *Answers:* 1. cry 2. rake 3. lace 4. cold 5. train 6. snail 7. jeep 8. feet 9. knight 10. nine.